Liberia's Son:
A True Story of Hope, Courage, and Resilience

Dave Verhaagen
with Yu-Jay Harris

A Hero House Publication

Liberia's Son:
A True Story of Hope, Courage, and Resilience

Hero House Publishing
6060 Piedmont Row Drive South
Suite 120
Charlotte, NC 28287
www.HeroHousePublishing.com

Text design by Sara Caitlyn Deal; Cover design by Zach Brown

Liberia's son/Dave Verhaagen with Yu-jay Harris

ISBN-13: 978-0-9965467-6-8

Acknowledgments

Every successful individual knows that his or her achievement depends on a community of persons working together. - Paul Ryan

This story is filled with unbelievable people God has blessed me to know over the course of my life. People like my remarkable mother, Rosetta, my wife and best friend, Nena, brother and best man, Jared, my hero uncle, Moses, the incredibly altruistic Taylors, dear friends like Carsten and Jamie, and others I remain grateful to for their pivotal role in shaping my life today. But there are so many more people, my mom, brother, and I have to thank for their prayers, advice, listening ears, encouragement, belief, coaching, and friendship over the course of our journey from the horrors of the Liberian Civil War to realizing the opportunities of life in the USA.

Our heartfelt thanks and gratitude to:

- **Mr. Eric Woods** – father, trusted friend, mentor, and so much more. You are a mighty good man.
- **Ms. Olivia Rashed** – the best mother-in-law on the planet – beautiful on the inside and out.
- **The Witherspoon family** – for lodging and taking care of mom when she made it to the Ivory Coast. We can't thank you enough!
- **The Larblah Family** – for making us your family without any reservations.
- **The Majors** – for your friendship and bravery helping mom to escape from Liberia.
- **Priscilla Walker and Family** – for hosting the three of us when we were in Abidjan applying for our travel Visas. The warmth of your home was very healing.
- **The Bowers and the Bowers Sunday School Class at First Baptist Church, Charlotte** – your prayers and kindness were uplifting during those early years as we settled in Charlotte.

- **Staff and parents of The Community School of Davidson** – for your continuous support of mom.
- **Family and friends in the Liberian community of Charlotte** – for your constant and dependable love over the years.
- **The Woods Family** – love and appreciate you all.
- **Leonard Satterwhite** – my friend, mentor, and someone who always believes in me.
- **Mr. Chris Martin** -- you were more than my advisor and English teacher at Country Day. You were and remain a dear friend and one of my biggest fans. A million thanks to you and Ms. Murphy for helping me get into college.
- **Mr. Sam Pennell** – your gregarious personality was contagious– and thankfully so. Thank you and your family for your love and friendship.
- **Hoonsuk Lee** – my incomparable friend
- **Roney Brown** – my friend and brother. You and your family are invaluable friends.
- **CCDS Posse** – Carsten, Mara, Jason, and Ian. You all made Country Day a time I'll never forget.
- **Kyle Ray** – you are my big brother, friend, and role model.
- **Melvin Ealey and Marin Meredith** – irreplaceable friends.

Special thanks to Dave Verhaagen, Ben Berg, Lauren Bordeaux, Sara Caitlyn Deal, Frank Gaskill and the entire team at Hero House Publishing/Southeast Psych. Working with you all on this book was a high moment in our lives. Thank you so much for this honor.

-Yu-jay

Map of Liberia

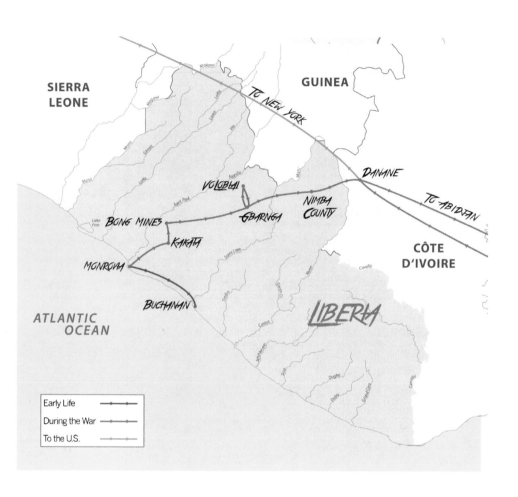

Access all videos included in this book

Contents

Foreword

I first met Yu-jay Harris over dinner years ago at a Chinese restaurant. He had asked to meet with me because he was seeking some parenting advice about his quickly expanding family. I was a psychologist and an author in the same town where he lived, and some mutual friends had given him my name because I had written a parenting book and spoke regularly on the topic. I later realized this was classic Yu-jay: collecting advice, gathering information from people who were knowledgeable in a particular subject area, planning ahead for the best possible outcome.

As soon as we sat down, I knew I was going to like this guy. He was incredibly warm and gregarious with a rare combination of interpersonal ease and intellectual intensity. I told my wife later that night, "You have to meet this guy. I could totally be good friends with him." This was only after about an hour of time with him. But in that hour, not only did I get the sense of what kind of man he was, but I got my first glimpse of his story. He told me about being from Liberia, Africa's oldest republic that had descended into a horrific civil war. He had escaped the war in the most breathtaking way imaginable and had become a remarkably accomplished man with a beautiful family, strong faith, good education from top tier schools, a successful professional career in corporate America, and a passion for mentoring. He had me hooked from the start.

I had long been emotionally attached to Liberia. Over a decade earlier, the Liberian Boys Choir had been in Charlotte performing at local churches to raise money and aware-

ness for orphans affected by the country's ongoing bloody civil conflict, a war that eventually took a quarter of a million
lives, created millions of refugees, and left countless others
physically and psychologically maimed and scarred. While
the boys were in town for their concert tour, their orphanage, a place in the jungle called Daniel Hoover Children's
Village, was overrun by armed rebels who ran their friends
and relatives out of their beds during the night at gunpoint.
The implications were immediately clear: the boys no longer
had a home. They couldn't be put back on a plane to return
to nothing. The families in the church where I heard the
concert, Christ Covenant in Matthews, North Carolina, an
adjoining town in the Charlotte area, rallied and several of
them took the boys in and petitioned to adopt them. Most of
these families had never dreamed of taking in an orphan—or
orphans—from a third world country and, in many cases,
they had to learn on the fly how to respond to the special
needs of these kids. These were kids who often had big
learning gaps, emotional struggles, adjustment challenges,
attachment issues, and, of course, lots of trauma exposure.
For many of these families, I became the go-to psychologist
to assess their kids' needs, consult with parents, or provide
therapy when needed. Some of the boys were surprisingly
intact, given what they had gone through. Others had deeper
struggles. Over the years, other families in the area who had
adopted Liberian kids came to me for support. I became close
with many of these families and remain so to this day.

The story of these Liberian boys and families was
so compelling that Oprah dedicated more than one show to
them over the years. My wife, Ellen, not knowing the full
extent of my involvement with the Liberian kids, watched
one of the shows and almost instantly felt a connection with

these kids. Later that week over dinner with another couple, she was talking about how she could see us adopting some Liberian kids. The woman cut a look at her husband. She proceeded to tell us of a situation she had become aware of where a local family had adopted two Liberian children and found out that their new daughter had two older siblings also living in the orphanage who were desperate to be adopted. We collected more information about them and talked it over with our teenage girls, both of them adopted at birth, and the consensus of the family was that we should move forward with the adoption. I now have four adopted children, including two Liberian siblings who live in the same city as their biological sister.

My connection with Liberia is deep. I've been there. I've been in the children's village you'll read about later that was overrun by rebels, sending terrified children into the streets as the soldiers fired submachine guns over their heads. I've met the President of Liberia, Ellen Sirleaf Johnson. I've consulted with her sister, Jennie Bernard, one of her senior advisors. I've visited nearly every location mentioned in this book in or around Monrovia (though I have not yet been out in the more remote countryside and the towns like Gbargna or the area of the refugee camp in Ivory Coast). I've been in the markets and on the beaches that were still strewn with piles of trash, in Kennedy Medical Center, and in government offices. The country with all its beauty and ugliness, its triumph and tragedy, has completely gotten under my skin. And this is mostly because of its people whom I find to be as lovely and wonderful as any people I've ever met in the world.

Yu-jay is one of those people. He's one of the most likable and impressive people I've ever met. When I decided to write a biography of a person who had demonstrated great resilience in the face of great hardship, he was at the top of my list. To my great delight, he was interested in collaborating with me. He had been told by many people that he had a story that needed to be shared, the kind of story that changes the people who hear it.

My research assistant, Ben Berg, was also enthused about the project. He set up numerous interviews with Yujay; his mother, Rosetta Woods; his brother, Jared Harris, as well as other players in this grand, real-life drama. Then he constructed the interviews into a timeline that I could use to write the book. There is no way this book would have been possible without him.

As you might suspect, the details from interviews, letters, emails, and news reports sometimes matched up well and other times did not, as each person remembers an experience in his or her own way. I went back later for follow-up interviews and re-read emails and letters to make sure the details and facts are as correct as possible. What you are about to read is a true story as accurate as it can be. I smoothed out some quotes and filled in some minor details, but it's all as true as possible. It's also a compelling and gripping story that is, by turns, heartbreaking and uplifting. And it's a story of resilience that will make you want to live a better life.

Dave Verhaagen
Charlotte, NC
November 1, 2015

PROLOGUE

The sun had just come up in Monrovia on a beautiful cloudless morning when government soldiers kicked in the door to Yu-jay's home. The eight armed men dressed in green camouflage military uniforms stormed through the house like a pack of rabid dogs, snarling and vicious and wild-eyed.

"Get up! Everyone outside!" they screamed. "Now!"

Yu-jay and his younger brother, Jared, along with their mother and grandmother, came out, arms up, squinting into the sun. They were joined by several adults the family had taken in for shelter during the civil war that had spread from 200 miles away in the countryside into the capital city of Monrovia. The jittery soldiers brandished M16 and AK-47 assault rifles as they lined up the terrified men, women, and children, nearly all stripped to their underwear. It was the first step of a mass murder.

At only 14 years old, Yu-jay understood he was probably going to die. He felt numb, almost as if his soul was already leaving his body. He became only flesh and bone now, already coming to terms with his imminent death. He made his peace with God, recalling a familiar Psalm: Lord, into your hands I commend my life.

These soldiers were on the run; the last men standing in their company. The rebels had beaten the government forces and were advancing on this remnant, pushing their way down the city streets; now this beautiful place, this coastal city, had descended into lawlessness and terror. They were men hardened from battle, but their eyes darted with fear and desperation. Their time was up. They knew they could rob these defenseless people, and then gun them down with no consequences. As soon as the rebels caught up with them, they'd all be dead men anyway. There was no hope for anyone here.

I didn't think I was supposed to die this young, 12-year-old Jared thought to himself.

"Who else is with you?" one of the soldiers barked at the line of civilians. They stood wordlessly, fearful and shivering, half-naked. Anxiety shot through the group. One other person, Fela, a Nigerian man who had become a close family friend, was hiding in the small, two-bedroom guesthouse to the left side of the main home Yu-jay lived in with his mom and brother. Fela had been in the small house when the soldiers arrived in the neighborhood. He ran to the main house to warn the others, then retreated back to the small house. During the brief time he was away alerting the family, the soldiers had taken the neighbors who lived in the house just behind where Fela was hiding and shot them dead. The armed men had apparently found bullet casings in the neighbor's home, which one of them had apparently been collecting, and accused them of being rebel sympathizers. They had killed two innocent people without a moment's hesitation. It was clear they intended to do the same thing here.

They knew it would be risky to expose Fela, but maybe even riskier to cover it up. If they lied, they'd all be dead when the men discovered Fela in the guest house; if they cooperated, maybe they'd have the slimmest of chances. There was no good choice here. Everyone sensed the soldiers were on the edge, unstable. These men were capable of anything. One misstep and this whole group of good men and women and even children could be gunned down in an instant. Finally, one of the men spoke.

"Come with me," he said. He led the soldiers to the little house where they rounded up Fela.

Some of the soldiers ransacked the two houses, gathering valuables into their bags and pockets. They took rings and gold necklaces and bracelets, jewelry Yu-jay's mother had been saving for her boys to give to their future wives. Now, it seemed likely there would be no future wives, no future children, no future. They took the Tissot watch Yu-jay had been given for his thirteenth birthday. It was his most prized possession. It scarcely mattered now.

Out front, there were 21 innocent people in all, completely dependent on the whims of these desperate armed men. Yu-jay's mother, Rosetta, kept the frightened group calm.

"We all need to pray," she told them.

The rebel gunfire grew closer and more intense. Yu-jay and the others knew their time was running out. If the soldiers didn't execute them, they would likely be caught in the crossfire of the coming battle and die anyway.

"Will you let us go back in the house?" Rosetta asked the man who appeared to be in charge. "And after the fighting is over, you can bring us back out and do whatever you want."

The man hesitated and eyed her with a steely stare. Their lives—all of them—hung in the balance of this hopeless man's decision.

"Yeah, go ahead" he said, then paused, "but I'm gonna throw a grenade in there."

They couldn't tell if he meant it—maybe he didn't even know—but all 21 of them quickly herded inside, aware of what certainly awaited them if they stayed out front.

The rebels soon arrived with gunshots and grenade bursts. The fighting raged throughout the neighborhood, up and down the streets. Inside, the terrified group crouched down away from the windows, but they could hear all of it. Gunfire and explosions, screams and yells. During this time, Yu-jay pleaded with God promising to live for Him if God would preserve him and his family. After three long, horrifying hours, it all stopped. There was an eerie silence. The once lively neighborhood, a place that had been filled with sounds of children playing and laughing, neighbors talking, dogs barking, birds chirping, even the chimes of an occasional ice cream truck, was now deadly quiet.

No one dared to move.

Finally, one of the men in the house slowly rose up and looked out the front window.

"The men are all gone," he said.

One by one, they slowly stood up and went outside.

They saw bodies everywhere. The soldiers, who just hours earlier had scared the family almost to death, lay about 50 yards away from the house, scattered about, some of them still clutching the loot they had stolen from Yu-jay's house in their hands.

"A dead body, that's something you'll never forget," Jared said later. "Never in your life."

The soldiers who had just hours earlier held all of their lives at the tips of their jumpy trigger fingers now laid lifeless on the ground. Yu-jay and a few others briefly considered taking back their things, meaning they literally would have to pry their belongings out of the hands of these dead men. They decided against it. The stuff was just not that important now.

In a lawless land, there would be no one to take the bodies away. In a few days, the stench would become unbearable. In reverence, the older men gathered the two bodies of the neighbors that had been killed next door, placed tires on them, doused the pile with gasoline and set it ablaze. No one dared to touch the soldiers' bodies because they were not close enough to the houses and everyone was too frightened to mess with them. So they left them there. These soldiers and a few rebels had lost their lives, but so had the survivors. For Yu-jay and his family, the life they once had was gone.

1

A SPECIAL DAY

"There are two great days in a person's life—the day we are born and the day we discover why."
- William Barclay

Yu-jay Harris turned 13 on April 26, 1989. It was a Wednesday on the coast of West Africa, an ordinary school day. Elsewhere in the world, there was trouble and turmoil—a huge tornado killed 1300 people and left another 80,000 homeless in Bangladesh and the rumblings of unrest in China's Tiananmen Square were just beginning—but in Monrovia, all was peaceful and calm. Yu-jay rose early and got dressed, just as he did on any other school day. He ate a bit of sweet cornbread his mom had made for breakfast before she took him to school that morning around 8:30. The school was St. Patrick's, perhaps the most prestigious school in the country, outside of the private American Cooperative School in Monrovia. St. Patrick's was a private, all boys, parochial Catholic school well known for its academic rigor and excellence

At St. Patrick's, everyone went to mass each Wednesday and this week was no exception. The students, all wearing the same uniform—khaki pants and white shirts with the school's badge sewn on the right pocket —filed into the small chapel to begin the service. Afterwards, they went to their classes, but no one mentioned Yu-jay's birthday. Birthdays were usually not that significant in Liberia, at least not enough to warrant public attention and celebration at school. The school day ended around 2:00 p.m. and Yu-jay slid into the back seat of a taxi his mom had hired to pick him and his brother up from school. Once home, he did his homework right away. Mom's rule was you could not play until all homework was finished. It was strictly enforced. On some days, he had an after-school tutor, and he would be done with all his homework before he even got home. But on this night, he still had some work to do before he could go out. When he was done, he hurried out to join the other kids for soccer and some ping-pong in the driveway on a makeshift ping-pong table—a plywood board with a net on top of two chairs.

There wasn't much distinction between the classes in this neighborhood full of families. Yu-jay and his family lived in a nice, eye-catching house, but right outside their door was a small shack that was home to another neighbor. And so it was throughout the neighborhood with the well-off and poor mixed together. The kids played with each other; their parents chatted and had dinners together. In America, the neighborhoods tend to be clearly separated by class, but this wasn't the case in Liberia. The lines between one class and another were evident in some ways, especially in the style of dress and where kids went to school, but these external differences were no barriers to relationship.

There was a feeling of safety in the neighborhood. It was virtually free of crime, with hardly any break-ins and certainly no violence. The nights were still, and before the kids arose for school, the mornings were full of the sound of chirping birds

"You didn't lock up your doors," Rosetta said, recalling the experience of living in that serene place. "People didn't kidnap kids and your neighbors could come in and out of your house. Your friends came in and out."

For the neighborhood kids, it was more out than in. They'd play soccer and other games until dark. Usually the only time they might come in during the daylight hours was to get a drink of water and escape the heat for a few minutes, then it was back outside to play. The kids stayed active and lean. Watching television around the clock or spending hours playing on a gaming console were not options.

Rosetta's house, a unique, seven-sided beauty, was the hangout for the rest of the neighborhood, adult and child alike. This house, the neighborhood's hub of activity, was a blessing that Rosetta and the boys didn't take for granted. A lot of struggle and hardship had gone into getting them into that house. Over the years, Rosetta managed to parlay her job with a German company to another job with the American Embassy in Liberia. The job afforded them even more income and allowed them to have even nicer things.

Learn More

"We were living such a wonderful life," she said.

Rosetta's generosity extended beyond the immediate family. She learned of a young man named Sylvester Yarpah whose father had fallen on hard times. His family had little means of support at the time, but his father desperately wanted Sylvester to complete his education. The boy was in the eighth grade at the time and was bright, capable, and full of promise.

Rosetta gladly took him in, like another one of his family members had done earlier in his life, and helped Sylvester finish his high school education. He quickly became like an older brother to Yu-jay and Jared and was considered a part of the family, which happens frequently in many African cultures. Families take others of lesser financial and educational means into their homes when they are in need and those individuals become part of the family. It was also typical in many African cultures for this "adopted" child to sleep on the floor in the house, but Rosetta would not consider it for Sylvester.

"I never let him sleep on the floor. I would sleep on the floor and let him sleep in the bed if we had guests." She believes her earlier hardships actually made her more aware of the need to treat all people with respect. "Because I was treated badly, I wouldn't turn around and say, 'Oh, because I was treated wrong, I should do it to someone else.' I was wronged, therefore I should do right by somebody else. Very important."

Sylvester remembers details of that time vividly. He recalls Yu-jay being very focused and attentive to details.

"He would read a lot," Sylvester said. "He would sit with his legs crossed and read." But it wasn't all work for the young boy. Yu-jay also had a great sense of fun and played a lot outside, according to Sylvester. He knew that rare mixture of intellectual curiosity and playfulness would serve him well in the years to come.

Sylvester remembers the beautiful, heptagon-shaped family home well: It was in a neighborhood where even the President of Liberia owned a guest house. There were two bedrooms and two bathrooms, as well as one living room, a dining room, and a kitchen. The outside was painted blue and white, while the inside was white. The house was well-decorated with lots of artistic touches, flowers and ornate bamboo. The boys' room had its own attached bathroom. The kitchen had modern appliances, nice cabinets, and an electric stove.

"Everything was very nice," Sylvester said, recalling all the details of the place, as if he were back there once again.

They all remember these days as being happy and fun days, but they were also busy, industrious times. Rosetta worked hard at her job, while Sylvester took care of the day-to-day responsibilities of raising the boys when he wasn't in school. Yu-jay and Jared were challenged by their classes, which were rigorous by any standard.

In addition to Sylvester, Rosetta had others she was helping live in the home. "Because I had a good job, other people would come live with me who were not family—some of them were family—and we all just packed in that house and helped each other."

Learn More

The full house gave the place a sense of energy and fun. The kids played together. Everyone ate together. It was a true community.

After a few hours of soccer and ping-pong on the night

of Yu-jay's birthday, the kids disbanded and went inside for the night. Yu-jay and Jared owned an Atari video game system they and their friends would sometimes play, but most of the time, they were all outside, so it often went untouched for days at a time, including on this night. Instead, he watched television with the family. In Monrovia, the TV didn't come on until about 6:00 p.m. each night. On late nights when there was no school the next day, the television would sometimes stay on until midnight when the Liberian National Anthem finally came on, followed by static and white noise for the rest of the evening.

"Our home was so much fun!" Yu-jay's mom, Rosetta recalled. "In the evenings, everyone would come into my room after dinner and homework to watch a little TV before going to bed. We would all squeeze on my king-size bed shoulder-to-shoulder. Sometimes we would even have friends over and all of us would be on the bed and floor watching my 13-inch TV! So much fun! We were a close knit family!"

Yu-jay recalls a time, when he was ten years old, when the family settled into his mom's room and watched the miniseries Jesus of Nazareth together. He vividly remembers being moved by the sufferings and sacrifice of Christ. The experience began his own personal journey of faith and embedded in his mind the importance of personal sacrifice and the willingness to persevere during intense suffering. He had no idea how important that would be for him with what was to come.

Most of the time, though, the time around the television was just a fun, bonding experience for the family. They would all climb into the bed and watch old American TV shows, like Sanford and Son. Rosetta would always watched the news at 6:00 p.m., keeping up-to-date on the events in the country and around the world.

When it was time to go to bed, the boys had their own bedroom with an adjoining bathroom. They arranged their beds in an L shape and often talked until one of them dropped off into sleep.

Most school days had this rhythm: wake up, brush your teeth and wash your face, eat, go to school, come home and do homework, go outside and play, then return home, take a bath, have dinner, and watch TV in the evening. Friday and Saturday nights were movie nights when the family would watch American movies. In particular, Yu-jay remembers watching Top Gun, Delta Force, and other action movies.

"The boys loved anything with Chuck Norris and anything action-packed. They watched Westerns and Charles Bronson movies, too," Rosetta said.

On Sundays, the family would always go to church. Afterwards, they would go across the street and eat hot dogs and ice cream for lunch. Then Yu-jay would have a Sunday devotional with a few friends. The days, both the weekdays and the weekends, had a normal, familiar pattern.

So Yu-jay's actual birthday, that Wednesday, was a normal day in nearly every respect. There was nothing unusual about it: no party, no special attention, because the plan was to celebrate his birthday the following Saturday when everyone was off from school. He was extremely excited.

"Yu-jay's thirteenth birthday was a big deal. It was all he talked about from sun up to sun down for the whole month of April," said Rosetta. "Every kid was excited about turning 13," she added.

The weekend couldn't come soon enough. When it finally arrived, the party did not disappoint. There was a big turnout with swarms of Yu-jay's family and neighborhood friends in attendance.

"Everyone was there," Rosetta said, "There were probably more adults than kids there."

Yu-jay laughed at this memory. "Mom has always had so many friends. Every celebration for us would be filled with more adults than our peers and friends. She was so loved by many," he said.

All of Rosetta's friends came, as well as aunts and uncles, including Uncle Moses, who would prove to be instrumental in Yu-jay's story in the weeks and months to come. But it wasn't just adults who attended the big event. Yu-jay's best friend from the neighborhood, a boy named Jehu, was there, along with other close friends, as well. The day was full of "food, family, and fun," as Rosetta recalled it. There weren't many balloons or decorations, but it was a day of celebration. The makeshift plywood ping-pong table was once again set atop the two kitchen chairs and the boys rotated in for matches. Other kids played soccer in the field next to the house. It was loud and fun and festive. The kind of party a 13-year-old boy hopes will be his.

The food that day included rice, potato greens, palm butter, fried chicken, cornbread, and even rice bread. Yu-jay's aunt made a cake they placed candles on and they sang "Happy Birthday." Yu-jay got some clothes and a few other fun presents, but the big gift of the year was the Tissot watch. Rosetta's boss had traveled to Germany on business and had personally picked out the watch as a special gift for Yu-jay. It wasn't until later they learned that Tissot was an expensive brand name, one that cost anywhere from a few hundred to over a thousand dollars. The gold watch had an analog face and a digital screen. It was a beautiful gift, one that Yu-jay loved and cherished. When he opened it, he beamed with joy, put it on, and wore it with great pride.

"I wanted to wear it every day," he recalls, "but I didn't because it was so special."

On this afternoon of his birthday celebration, there were rumors of war, but nothing strong or reliable enough to warrant messing up a good party. Some people in town had family members living in more remote areas who heard the war was coming to their villages and had fled to the city. However, no one in Monrovia had seen anything to suggest a developing civil war. BBC News would talk about "the war in Liberia," but the Liberian broadcasts continued to assure them everything was fine. Rosetta and most of the others in town chose to believe the hometown reports over the British reports, especially since they saw no evidence of it. Surely the Liberian press would know better than the British news services. Besides, if there was a war brewing in the countryside, it would burn out before it ever reached the city. There was no chance it would ever make it all the way to the capital city. They all believed they were safe. It wasn't a time for worry. It was a time for celebration.

"We had no clue it was coming," Rosetta said. "No clue."

By the time they realized it was on their doorstep, it would be too late.

2

THE PROMISE OF FREEDOM AND HOPE

"If your dreams do not scare you, they are not big enough."
- Ellen Johnson Sirleaf, President of Liberia

Liberia is a beautiful country, nestled along the western coast of the Atlantic Ocean. It is bordered by Ivory Coast to its east, Sierra Leone to its west, and Guinea to its north. Dense thickets of mangroves, tropical shrubs with thick above-ground roots, line the coastline of Liberia. In the more sparsely populated interior, dense, tangled forests open up onto a plateau of dry plains and grasslands. The longest river in the country, the Cavalla, traverses 320 miles across the countryside and dumps into the Gulf of Guinea in the port town of Harper, one of the first towns settled by freed American and Caribbean slaves and home to a college, a hospital, and several secondary schools.

The capital city of Monrovia is home to nearly a quarter of the country's entire population of 4 million residents. The rest of its citizens are dispersed among more rural parts of the country, still largely separated by tribal affiliations.

English is its official language, but there are 31 indigenous languages spoken by the various tribes that make up the country. Most Liberians, though, speak some dialect of English, known collectively as Liberian English. It's a beautiful dialect, but one that is difficult for English speakers outside of West Africa to understand with its melodic cadences, partial pronunciations, and indigenous expressions.

"Ah hol ya foo," you might hear a Liberian child say to a parent or a teacher. It translates: "I hold your foot," which means, in essence, "I grovel before you. I beg your forgiveness."

You would say, "Mah ah can be turnee," if you got dizzy. It translates, "My eyes can be turning."

In Liberia, a "butter pear" is an avocado, "craw-craw" is a bad skin condition, and a person who is sick or undernourished is "dry."

Liberia is a proud African country, rich with culture and tradition. Its literary history goes back a full century. The country is also well-known for its quilt work and art. Two of the titans of American entertainment, Oprah Winfrey and Michael Jackson,

Learn More

have connections to the country. Oprah has traced her own ancestry back to the coastal African country, while the king

of pop paid tribute to it in song. In 1987, Michael released a single from his best-selling album Bad called "Liberian Girl." The video featured an all-star line-up of Hollywood celebrities, including John Travolta, Whoopi Goldberg, Steven Spielberg, and about three dozen other famous faces. The reaction in the country was a combination of shock and delight. Margaret Carson, a Liberian woman, told the Washington Times, "The Liberian girls were so astonished to hear a great musician like Michael Jackson thinking about a little country in Africa."

Liberia's unique cuisine includes pepper soup, cassava leaf, fish, and plantains, all usually served over a bed of rice or fufu, a yellowish, starchy dough made of cassava, yam, or potatoes. Soccer—there called football, of course—is far and away the most popular sport in Liberia. The Liberian national football team has twice reached the Africa Cup of Nations, and Liberian George Weah is the only African to be named FIFA World Player of the Year.

Yu-jay and his family were fully immersed in all aspects of Liberian culture, from the meals they cooked to the art that decorated their home to their love for football. At the time of his thirteenth birthday party, they would never suspect that all of this rich tradition would be upended within the year. Just as the foreign news reports had said, fighting had recently begun in the remote regions, far away from the capital city, and the long-simmering conflict would soon reach Monrovia, much faster than anyone would have ever guessed. But the powder keg of civil war that was just beginning to explode out in the countryside was nothing new. It had been smoldering for over a century.

To fully understand the civil war, you have to understand the origins of the country itself. It actually began in the American South during the early 1820s with the help of a private organization called the American Colonization Society. The ACS had favor with prominent and influential politicians like James Monroe and Henry Clay, and even, for a while, Abraham Lincoln. These individuals all believed that repatriation back to Africa was a preferable option to emancipation in the United States. The belief was that these former slaves would have greater opportunity and safety in a new, free land on the coast of Africa. In essence, ACS created Liberia to resettle slaves instead of having them freed and growing in population in the U.S. because the predominant belief was that a large group of freed slaves posed a threat to the country.

In 1847, this new country officially became the Republic of Liberia, setting up a democratic model of government patterned after that of the United States. The name Liberia means "land of the free," an idea echoed in the country's national anthem and pledge of allegiance. The capital city was called Monrovia, named after President James Monroe who was a vocal proponent of colonization. These freed slaves and their descendants were known as Americo-Liberians and though they comprised less than 3% of the country's entire population, they took prominent positions of power and influence in politics, business, and culture because of the skills and experiences they brought from the US. Though technically a democracy, these colonists and their descendants ruled Liberia for more than 130 years. The first president of Liberia, Joseph Jenkins Roberts, was born in Virginia and though he was considered to be a black man, he could have easily passed for a white person. He was apparently only one-eighth black.

Early in the country's history, the ruling party passed a law prohibiting foreign trade with the inland tribes, severely curtailing the economic growth of those groups of people. Indigenous Africans were not even allowed to become citizens for more than half a century after the country was founded. It is a curious aspect of human nature that those who had been deprived of basic rights in turn did the same to others. The former slaves who were mistreated and severely discriminated against in America did the same thing to their fellow country people in their new land. Because of this, the Americo-Liberians were often met with strong and violent opposition from the other African groups in the country. The seeds of resentment and strife between this powerful minority ruling class and the indigenous people were planted early.

In 1917, Liberia joined the United States by entering into the First World War, declaring war on Germany. The action gave the Allies a much-needed base in West Africa and won favor with many Americans and Europeans. The war was settled the following year, but it put the small African country onto the world stage for the first time in the modern era.

Less than a decade later, in 1926, the Firestone Tire and Rubber Company opened a large rubber producing plant on land granted by the government of Liberia. The economic effect on the country was enormous. Rubber manufacturing quickly became one of the backbones of the young country's developing economy and Firestone became a major player in Liberia for decades to come.

During World War II, the U.S. was granted a military base in Liberia that was used for fueling and maintaining planes fighting in North Africa. There were accounts that Hitler considered bombing the base in Liberia but thought it was scarcely worth the effort after he realized the tip of his pinky finger was covering up the entire country of Liberia on the map he was using. His decision to back off gave the Allies a surprising advantage.

In 1943, Liberia elected William Tubman president. A direct descendant of liberated U.S. slaves, but born in Liberia, Tubman grew up in abject poverty. His father was a strict disciplinarian and it is reported that he made William and his four siblings sleep on the floor because he believed beds were too soft and would lead to a softness of moral character. When he became president at the age of 48, Tubman instituted broad and sweeping reforms, many of them well ahead of their time, including the establishment of a public school system. During this era, under his leadership, Liberia began to modernize, constructing the Freeport of Liberia, a large commercial port on Bushrod Island off the coast of Monrovia, along with an international airport, both built by U.S. workers through a cooperative venture between the two countries. The growing African republic also found its footing on the international scene, becoming a founding member of the United Nations in 1945 and speaking out strongly against South African apartheid and in favor of African independence from European colonization. Tubman and his allies envisioned an increasingly unified Africa. Liberia became one of the founding nations of the Organization of

African Unity, founded in 1963 to promote solidarity across Africa and to foster mutually beneficial economic growth. It even introduced a single African currency that could be used across the continent, in much the same way that the European Union introduced the Euro many decades later. Tubman also shrewdly encouraged foreign investment in Liberia, generating the second-highest economic growth rate of any country in the world during the 1950s. By then, the country had grown to nearly 3 million people.

It was also during the 1950s that the country saw significant progress in its own civil rights. In May of 1951, thanks to the efforts of Tubman, women and indigenous property owners were given the right to vote in the presidential election for the first time. Seven years later, all forms of racial discrimination were officially outlawed. In many ways, the country far outpaced not only other African countries, but also many Western countries in its pursuit of equality and fairness.

The country saw four decades of modern growth and prosperity. Over that span of time, Liberia had a generally well-functioning government and a thriving business environment. The country had developed a power grid, paved roads and highways, built stores and supermarkets, ran a postal service, and many of its citizens, including Yu-jay and his family, had all of the conveniences of modern life.

In 1979, the first hints of discord boiling under the surface of the beautiful country bubbled up when forty people were killed in riots following a proposed increase in the price of rice, the staple of the people's daily diet. The terrifying riots ushered in an era of fear and instability. The following year, a Master Sergeant in the Liberian Army named Samuel K. Doe, or SKD as he was known in Liberia, carried out an audacious military coup of the government. Tubman's successor, President William Tolbert, then 66 years old, was killed in his sleep, and 13 of his aides were publicly executed. Doe suspended the constitution and assumed full powers of control over the country. His People's Redemption Council became a single-party ruling government for four years until they were pressured by the international community to allow opposition candidates. But even the opposition parties knew not to press Doe too hard. Any threat to his seat of power was met with swift and bitter repercussions. After a failed coup in which soldiers briefly held the national radio station, Doe's government retaliated by brutally slaughtering members of the Mano and Gio tribes, where many of the plotters came from. In 1985, after a new constitution had been adopted, Doe won the presidential election, though most outside governments condemned this and viewed subsequent elections as fraudulent.

Four years later on Christmas Eve of 1989, a man named Charles Taylor, a former politician and government official in Samuel Doe's administration, and his National Patriotic Front of Liberia began a serious uprising against the government. By September of 1990, Taylor's forces had gained control of nearly the entire country, with the exception of a small area just outside of Monrovia, which was held by Doe's remaining military. After bloody fighting, Doe was captured and executed within the month by Prince Johnson, one of Taylor's top former commanders who had splintered from the original rebel group. SKD's demise was videotaped, showing Johnson's soldiers surrounding the former president and cheering as he was tortured and executed.

But the rebels soon split into several warring factions, each battling the others for control of the country. From 1989, the year of Yu-jay's thirteenth birthday, until 1996, the country would descend into a brutal, nightmarish civil war that would kill more than 200,000 Liberians and displace more than a million others. This was only the first of two horrible civil wars that would consume the country.

3

WAR AT HOME

"Forget what hurt you in the past, but never forget what it taught you. However, if it taught you to hold onto grudges, seek revenge, not forgive or show compassion, to categorize people as good or bad, to distrust and be guarded with your feelings then you didn't learn a thing."
- Shannon Adler

While war was brewing in the countryside as Yu-jay was becoming a teenager, his family, which had since become peaceful and happy, had its own history of conflict and strife. A casual observer at Yu-jay's birthday party would have seen the fun-loving and happy family, the upscale house, the privilege of private school, and all the other indications of success and have no idea of the hardship that had gone into creating this life. But for Rosetta, the matriarch of this family, getting to this point was anything but easy.

"I was born in the village in Grand Bassa County," she began, as she told the story of her family's roots.

Grand Bassa is a remote county about three to four hours away from Monrovia. In Liberia, the counties are like little states, each with their own capitals. Grand Bassa county is one of 15 counties in Liberia and the fifth most populous. It's home to a large iron-ore mining operation that is currently managed by Arcelo-Mittal, the world's largest steel producer. Grand Bassa covers over 3,000 square miles, which is slightly bigger than the state of Delaware, but Rosetta was born in the heart of the county in a tiny village virtually cut off from the rest of the world.

As a young child, Rosetta had no idea there was a bigger world out there. All she knew was her parents, grandparents, and the small village around her, including the small church where her father was the pastor. Being isolated had its advantages. Since the village was the only thing she knew, she didn't feel poor, despite living in conditions that would be considered extreme poverty in most other parts of the world. To this day, she recalls the little village with affection.

Learn More

"I was happy, playing. We were really creative with play. We came up with our own games and made our own dolls," she said. "I don't look at the time in the village as something to be sad about. It was some of the happiest times of my life because I was with family. I was secure. I ate whenever I wanted to eat."

It's true that they ate whenever they wanted, but it wasn't because they had a single market or grocery store. They ate well because they grew their own food on a farm where they labored hard from early in the morning through the heat of the day and sometimes into the evening. They truly worked for their supper. Despite the grueling work, Rosetta recalled no complaining among the adults or even the other children. It was what needed to be done, so everyone did their share.

Her only link to the outside world was a small transistor radio her dad kept. Every night they would listen to the news out of Buchanan, the capital of Grand Bassa country, broadcasted in Bassa, the local dialect, then turn it off to save the batteries. When the batteries eventually died, her dad would boil the batteries in water, then lay them out in the sun to dry. Once dry, he would put them back in the radio and they would work like new, at least for a while. They had enough battery power to allow them to hear the news for the next several evenings.

When Rosetta was still a child, her older brother came to the village to ask her parents if Rosetta could come to Buchanan, where he and other members of the family lived. Joe was in Buchanan pursing his high school diploma and working part time at the local hospital as a laboratory technician. He had made arrangements for her to live with Mrs. Wells, a colleague from work, and her family. She would be his responsibility and have the opportunity to pursue her education. The older siblings had long since moved to Buchanan and Monrovia where there were many more opportunities for school and work. When he told her of this possibility, she remembers thinking, Who is in the city? What is the city? She had no idea what it could even mean. The city might as well have been on the other side of the world. For Rosetta, it was almost like a make-believe land, something she couldn't even imagine.

After a great deal of deliberation, her parents finally agreed and allowed her to move to Buchanan with her brother to live with the Willis family. She was only eight years old at the time and she remembers feeling terrified.

"I left my father, my mother, my security. I didn't know a word of English. I had seen missionaries come to our village. I didn't know who they were because I didn't know there were other races in the world, so I was scared to death, you know," she said.

Buchanan opened up new possibilities for young Rosetta. She remembers seeing a car for the first time and her brother told her they were going to get inside of it and it was going to take them places. You get inside of that and it takes you places? She could scarcely wrap her head around any of this. It was hard to take it all in.

"The only thing that I knew was a canoe because we

would get in it and cross the river. That's it. I didn't know anything else," she explained.

But Rosetta's wide-eyed adventure to the city took a dark turn. Mrs. Wells and her husband were eccentric people. Mr. Wells, for example, would frequently dress up in a cowboy hat and boots and parade around. Rosetta had little contact with him, though. Instead, it was Mrs. Wells, a nurse who worked at a nearby clinic, who ran the house.

No one suspected this woman's home would end up being a hellish experience for young Rosetta, full of abuse and deprivation. Rosetta still did not speak English at the time and when she could not understand Mrs. Wells, the woman would beat her badly.

"I would say no when I was supposed to say yes. I got a lot of beatings. I had welts all over me," Rosetta recalled.

She also remembered being locked in a room for days for not understanding the woman or being able to communicate with her.

"The neighbors would put food on a piece of paper and give it to me because they knew I was in there and I was hungry. When she wasn't looking I would open the window and ask them for food."

Instead of trying to return to her parents' village or contact her brother, she stayed and suffered through the mistreatment and abuse. She stayed partly because she was powerless to do otherwise, but partly because she believed it was the only way to get an education.

"Just to be able to read and write," she said.

But despite having left the village to go to school and enduring the beatings and neglect, she still wasn't getting the education she expected. Instead, she was caught in a trap of indentured servitude, much like in fairytales like Cinderella, except this was no make-believe. This was Rosetta's life from the age of eight until she was eleven. For three full years she put up with abuse and mistreatment. On some good days she would go to school, but on other days, Mrs. Wells would keep her home to clean the house. On worse days, she would beat her.

"There was a lot of work into the late night and I slept on the ground, on the cement floor lying on a few of my dresses. I would make a pallet and sleep on there at night and if it rained, it would come right through the house. And there was nobody to complain to."

Learn More

While enduring the mistreatment—being locked in the room, sleeping on the cold concrete floor, the forced labor, the beatings—for those three long years, she pushed herself to learn to read. She knew her parents had allowed her to go to the city to be able to read and write and do math, but she found she had to do most of it herself.

"I practiced my letters in the dirt with my finger or stick," she said. "I would use that and learn how to write, learn my numbers and my letters, addition, and subtraction. I did all that in the dirt because I didn't have enough paper to practice as often as I wanted."

Later she taught herself how to type on a keyboard with no formal instruction. She was constantly pushing herself to learn. Even today, much later in life, she describes herself as an avid reader hungry for education.

"If I could go to school, I would go to school. I really would go to school," she said.

Her parents didn't come to visit her very often for fear that she would want to go back with them. Unaware of her abusive situation, they wanted her to stay in the city where she could get an education, learn to read and write, and have opportunities they didn't have. If you did that, they told her, you could get a good job. Had her parents known of her nightmarish conditions, they might have taken her back to the village and her life would have turned out very differently, perhaps in some ways for the better, but possibly in other ways for the worse.

After those three long years, she finally left Mrs. Wells and her cowboy husband to live temporarily with her sister and her family. A few months later, she would move yet again to live with another family, Mr. and Mrs. Cotts. Mr. Cotts was a professional tailor and Mrs. Cotts stayed at home and took care of the house and their two children. They viewed Rosetta much the same way as Mrs. Wells had. She was disregarded and neglected and experienced nearly the same treatment she had suffered at the hands of her previous caretaker. It became apparent the Cottses had no interest in taking care of Rosetta or in educating her. She was there simply to work as a servant. So she lived in miserable circumstances and worked much of the time. All the while, she was still teaching herself to read. As with the Wells family, she ended up staying with the Cotts family for nearly three full years, enduring the neglect for even a glimmer of hope for an education.

When Rosetta was thirteen, her brother Joe, the one who had originally brought her into the city, got married. His life was now established—having completed his education, landed a good job at the Census Bureau in Buchanan, and gotten married—and now able to make good on his original promise, the one he had made over five years earlier. Joe and his wife invited Rosetta into their home in Buchanan and she became almost like their child.

"We were so close," she recalled.

Joe and his wife took her in for five years and made sure she got a real education. Not only did Joe get her into a good private school, but he also checked over her notes, checked her spelling, and ensured she understood what she was being taught.

After some time, her parents were also able to move to Buchanan. It seemed like a great moment because nearly all the family was back together or at least nearby, but the older couple never quite fit in. Being from the remote village, they were culturally at odds with urban life. Their English wasn't strong and they were unaccustomed to the faster pace of the city. Rosetta's father made charcoal to sell and tried to help the family any way he could, but he died within a few years of arriving in the city when Rosetta was still only in her teens.

Despite the turmoil and the family struggles, Rosetta pushed herself hard in school. She was not only smart, but she was tough-minded and possessed the kind of grit and determination that allowed her to overcome terrible mistreatment and hardship. It was this same unwavering style that served her well in the challenges she would encounter down the road.

While in her late teens, she learned information that would change her life forever: she found out she was pregnant with Yu-jay. She was an unwed teen mom with no job and not many prospects. The news was not received well by her family. Joe was especially enraged at her. He yelled at her, saying she had wrecked her life.

"He really wanted me to go to finish high school," she explained.

People in town didn't hold back from expressing their disdain either. "People were upset and said a lot of things. You know, teenage pregnancy and all that," she said. Their judgments were hurtful to her.

"You know, all the things that come, all the words and disappointment that come with it, I had to endure that," she said.

She persevered and gave birth to Yu-jay on April 26, 1976. He was born in a hospital in Buchanan built by the now-defunct Liberian-American-Swedish Minerals Company, or LAMCO, a corporation that would cease operations during the coming civil war. For now, though, the country was at peace as Yu-jay came into the world. For Rosetta, as difficult and gut-wrenching as the experience had been for her to be pregnant, she knew this child was special from the beginning.

"I cannot see my life without him, ever. He's a gift."

Rosetta was from the Bassa tribe, the second largest ethnic group in the country, so she chose a Bassa name for him. She named him Yu-jay, which means, "for the sake of this child." His name is rife with meaning.

"You know, for the sake of this child, I had to endure hardship. I had to go hungry. I had to cut my education short. I had to forgo my dreams. For the sake of this child," she explained. "It was just the right name for him. He couldn't have been named any other name."

From the time he was an infant, Rosetta and Yu-jay had a tight bond, one that got them through the toughest of times, including times when they were destitute and hungry and times when they feared for their lives. It was the kind of attachment that is forged in the worst kinds of adversity. Yu-jay has described himself

Learn More

as a "momma's boy" who was very close to his mother, but he had no other choice. He was a sickly kid, asthmatic, prone to illness. He needed her to get through the worst of times.

"I took care of him. If I was in the home, he was with me. And everywhere I went, he was with me," she said.

Despite the struggles—or maybe because of them—Rosetta and Yu-jay were inseparable when he was a younger child. When he was only a few months old, they moved from Joe's home in Buchanan to Monrovia, where her parents had moved to pursue a better life. In the city, Rosetta and Yu-jay rented a small room in the home of a family friend. The house was built with cement blocks, unpainted, and had a zinc-lined roof. Rosetta and her infant son lived in the room that was approximately 8 feet by 10 feet in size, had one light bulb, a window, and no bathroom, which forced Rosetta to use an outhouse. Of course, there was no air-conditioning and not even a fan. It was essentially one level up from being homeless and living on the street. The rent was seven dollars a month, but even that was too high for the struggling family. Rosetta was a young mom who was trying to continue her schooling, having progressed to the seventh grade. She had no means of support and would often have to beg family and friends to help her pay the rent. Often they were months behind.

Rosetta needed a job. While she searched in vain for work, she made the hard decision to let Yu-jay go and live with his paternal grandparents back in Buchanan, about 85 miles away. Jared, who was born a few years after Yu-jay, went to live with Rosetta's mother. After five years of struggling, she found a job working as a teacher at a pre-school where she was able to sleep on a military camp bed in the kitchen, which was sectioned off from the rest of the school.

And though money and housing were huge stressors for Rosetta, she never found Yu-jay to be a burden. Even as a young child, she recalls, he was easy-going and compliant.

"I had to tell him just once and he would do it," she said.

Even with the hardships of being a teen mom with practically no income and poor living conditions, Rosetta drew upon her grit and determination, scraping by until she was eventually able to graduate from high school. By that time, she was 23 years old with two young boys. She couldn't imagine her life without them. She loved her boys deeply and wanted to give them her very best. Her persistence paid off. Her diploma allowed her to secure a position working with Brawico, a German-owned general store. At the time, it was a godsend for her.

"They treated me like family," she said of her employer.

She worked hard for them and they paid her well, so she was able to build her own house—her dream house—with two bedrooms and two baths. One bedroom was for the boys and the other bedroom was for her. Recalling their time in the house, all of them—Rosetta, Jared, and Yu-jay—think of it fondly. "It was just wonderful," Rosetta said. "We loved being together and laughing and watching movies and just living."

They had built a great life for themselves. Rosetta had overcome the odds, finished school, and had gotten an excellent job that allowed her to build her own house, get a car, and even put her boys in private school. She did all of this as a single mom born to a poor, rural family in a remote village, a woman who endured abuse and neglect, a person who had taught herself

Learn More

to read by scratching out letters on a dirt floor. By sheer willpower and determination, she had created a better life for herself and her boys. At long last, her life was good and joyful.

"It was just really, really, really happy," she said with a broad smile, then she paused for a moment, lost in thought. "Really happy."

4

MOSES, THE DELIVERER

"Leaders lead but in the end it's the people who deliver."
- Tony Blair

Moses Gibson was a short, stocky Liberian man with a dark complexion, a quick wit, and a joyfully devilish personality. He was more than an ordinary man, though. There was something remarkable about him. Nearly everyone who met him sensed it. He was different than most, as if he were chosen for a higher purpose, a bigger calling. Maybe it was the force of his strong and passionate personality. Maybe it was physical fierceness. But maybe it was something more.

Rosetta first met Moses on a business trip to Ivory Coast where she traveled occasionally to buy various items including fabric, artwork, and clothing she would resell back in Monrovia. , She traveled with a friend, and unfortunately, neither of them spoke French, which was a necessity to do business in the former French colony with a stable, trade-driven economy. An acquaintance at the embassy told them of a Liberian man he knew who spoke English, but was also fluent in French (and several Liberian dialects, to boot) and could help them navigate the market and negotiate the things they wanted to buy. They were thrilled at the prospect of having someone translate for them and, even more importantly, having someone who knew the culture.

The man introduced her to Moses. He and Rosetta hit it off immediately, having an easy rapport with each other. He made her laugh and he had a mesmerizing presence.

"What are you doing here in Ivory Coast?" Rosetta asked him in English during their trip to the market.

"I wanted to go to America," Moses said. "I came to see if I could get a visa to go there, but I have been waiting here three, four years and nothing is happening."

"You are still young," Rosetta replied playfully. "Come back to Liberia and stay at my house and get on your feet."

This was an African custom. If you met someone who had a need and you could meet that need, you offered to take them into your home and make them part of your family. This was especially true for Rosetta who practiced hospitality that far exceeded even traditional Liberian generosity.

A few months later, Moses would accept her offer and return to Liberia to live with Rosetta, who became like an adopted big sister. He ended up staying

Learn More

in the house rent-free for three years. Rosetta told him that whatever money he earned was his to keep so he could get on his feet.

Yu-jay was eight-years-old when Moses moved in. The man became so close to the family that the boys began to call him Uncle Moses. This wild, adventurous man fascinated Yu-jay. He had a magnetic personality that drew people in. He was also a first-degree black belt in Tae Kwon Do, had received his training in Korea, and did some competitive fighting in Liberia for a period of time. Like most boys who grew up on Chuck Norris movies, Yu-jay and Jared were fascinated with martial arts, so Moses gave them formal Tae Kwon Do lessons for about a year. He would take the boys out and show them the moves. Even at the time, Yu-jay could tell it was obvious Moses knew what he was doing. He was not a man to be trifled with.

"He was the guy you always felt safe around because he could pretty much whoop anyone's butt," Yu-jay said. "No one's gonna mess with him. I wouldn't."

Yet Moses was a complex person who was tough and even ferocious at times, but he could also be gentle and warm. He was a joyful man with a big laugh. Yu-jay and Rosetta both remember his wicked sense of humor.

"He's hilarious. If he were here in the U.S., he would

be a comedian like Chris Rock or Eddie Murphy. He is so funny. He was crazy, but very fun," she recalled.

Moses had a big personality and a massive appetite. He was constantly consuming huge amounts of food. When he came over for meals, there were no leftovers because Uncle Moses was sure to eat everything. He came up with a contest he called "The Black Snake Society." The rules were that if you didn't eat your food, he'd eat it.

"Of course, he always won," Yu-jay added.

When Rosetta first met him, he had been a little down on his luck, but Moses was a remarkably resourceful man who always seemed to land on his feet, even when he was in a jam. He had a knack for figuring out ways to make money and had no qualms about how he did it.

"He would take a dollar from an 8-year-old," Yu-jay said laughingly. "If you had money, he would take it away from you. He would come up with a way. He wasn't like a jerk who would take it by force, but he would come up with a way, something that sounds so exciting and you would say, 'Okay, here you go. Here's five bucks I just got.'"

Moses' ability to sense financial opportunities and seize the exact right moment would come in handy during the war to come. By the time the rebels took over the town of Bong Mines, he had established a Tae Kwon Do school in the area. Some of Charles Taylor's troops who knew Moses and his work as a martial arts expert recommended him to the rebel leader to be part of Taylor's security detail and train the rebels in hand-to-hand combat techniques. Moses sensed the opportunity and took the offer, a move that would become invaluable to Yu-jay's family in ways they could have never foreseen. His choice to be part of Charles Taylor's retinue was not driven by any sort of political ideology. It was simply a pragmatic decision on Moses' part to pay the bills.

"I always thought that he wanted to use the opportunity to help his family," Yu-jay said.

Moses' charisma and personal influence would later allow him to become a man of power and influence in the rebel army, training the soldiers in hand-to-hand combat and serving close to Taylor himself. His rare combination of physical prowess, charm, and cunning ensured that he would be a valuable asset to the group that wanted to overthrow the current Liberian government. He had no idea all of these things would also be the only hope of saving the lives of Yu-jay, Jared, and Rosetta.

The ancient biblical story of Moses is one of a special man who, despite great odds and risks to his life and safety, leads his people out of oppression and into freedom and safety. Moses Gibson would soon play that same role for Yu-jay and his family.

5

RUMORS OF WAR

"What a cruel thing war is, to fill our hearts with hatred instead of love for our neighbors."
- Robert E. Lee

By the middle of 1989, the war was swirling deep in the bush. It was soon to engulf the country like a gathering storm, devastating everything in its path on its way to the capital city. This was no ordinary war. It was brutal and ruthless and terrifying. Had anyone in Monrovia really known what was going on in the remote areas, they would have all run for their lives.

Because the media was essentially state-run, most of the citizens of Monrovia had no idea how crushed in defeat the Liberian army, known as AFL (the Armed Forces of Liberia), had been in the earlier countryside battles. The people were all being told about minor skirmishes but were left with the impression that it was all under control and going to blow over soon. Occasionally, Yu-jay's family would get news from friends in the U.S. who heard on BBC and other international outlets that the rebel forces were capturing one city after another. Despite this, there was no evidence that the fighting posed any risk of reaching the capital.

"As a 12 or 13-year-old kid, I never felt any sort of danger or concern for my part," Yu-jay said.

His perception was not uncommon. At the time, most of the citizens of the big city were scarcely concerned with the little dust-ups that were happening out in the distant jungle areas.

The war came in like a gathering storm with rumblings in the distance and then louder booms closer and closer, but nearly everyone in the capital city, including Yu-jay and his family, were caught completely off-guard by it.

"In America, if there is a hurricane coming or some adverse weather, you know. You have all these ways of knowing. It's big in the media that there's a storm coming. There is none of that in Liberia. It just sort of happened," Yu-jay explained. "It wasn't like we knew something was coming and we stockpiled food and water—which we would have done if we had early warnings. We did not. It just sort of came at us."

One day, about six or seven people who lived on the outskirts of the city came to Yu-jay's house, saying nervously, "The rebels have come. There is fighting all around our neighborhood!" All of them were running to find shelter. Rosetta immediately took them in.

The first hint of panic set in as the family sat around the dinner table and heard their friends describe the gun-fights down their street. It sounded surreal, like something that could never happen in the city. Still, the media continued to say everything was under control. No need for worry.

The storm of war had slowly begun to shut down the city. Their school closed. Stores closed. It was hard to find food. And because their household had swollen from six to about 21 people, the family had to ration carefully. They would let the little rice they had soak for hours before cooking, a process that caused the rice to swell and feed more people – though it was barely filling. They began eating only once a day and only small amounts.

The Sunday after the other family sought shelter in their home, Rosetta left early for church in a taxi, having put Yu-jay and Jared in the care of her nephew. The three of them would follow her later in another taxi because she had to get there early that morning to meet a friend of hers at church who was coming from America. It would be good to see her old friend again.

As the taxi sped down the road toward the church, a large truck, an older WWII U.S. military truck refurbished for use in Liberia, loaded with soldiers, barreled toward them and crossed into their lane, slamming head-on into the taxi with a sickening explosion of glass and metal.

Rosetta, sitting in the front of the cab, was hit with the full force of the impact. There were no airbags. Hardly anyone wore seatbelts. The car crumpled around her, mangling her ankle and snapping her collarbone. She was pinned in the car, bleeding profusely and in intense pain.

Learn More

The government soldiers, maybe aware they were about to be overthrown by the more powerful rebel army, had been out looting people's houses and had a large freezer they had stolen in the back of the truck. The extra weight made the impact even more powerful. The soldiers fled the scene but some on lookers ran to a nearby house and got an ax. They chopped through the car to get Rosetta out.

"I really thought I was dead," she said. "It was by the grace of God. I felt myself dying because I saw the car coming and I was in the front. No seat belts, so it's a miracle that I survived."

Once they finally cut her out of the car, they flagged down another passing taxi and lay down the seats to get her inside and off to the hospital. The taxi sped there as quickly as it could. Once she arrived, her whole body racked with excruciating pain, they found no doctors there, no medicine, no help at all. The hospital staff had all abandoned the town now engulfed with rebel soldiers. Her foot was badly twisted and mangled, but all anyone could do was tie up cardboard around it and send her to another hospital.

Once she arrived at the next hospital, Kennedy Medical Center, the largest hospital in the country, they found there were no doctors there either, and the electricity flickered off and on, announcing the start of the war. Other family members met them there and went out looking in vain for doctors. She had no doctors and no medicine and she laid there in agonizing pain.

"I'm crying 24 hours until there were no more tears because I am in excruciating pain," she recalled.

Finally, after two days of languishing in the near-ghost town of a hospital, a doctor who worked with her at the U.S. Embassy came to Kennedy Medical Center and signed her out so she could be brought to another hospital, ELWA, which stands for Eternal Love Winning Africa, a hospital founded in 1965 by American Christian missionaries. It is the same hospital that was at the forefront of the fight against Ebola in more recent years. She ended up staying at the missionary hospital for a full week. It was a week of excruciating pain. When the swelling in her foot finally went down, they were able to do an initial surgery. Almost immediately after that, though, the doctor urged her to leave the hospital early because the rebels were likely to overrun the hospital at any moment. She hurried home that Sunday afternoon and ate her first real meal in more than a week. She needed to eat and rest. But it was early the next morning, Monday, when the government soldiers would bust through her front door.

6

WAR COMES TO TOWN

"All wars are civil wars because all men are brothers."
- François Fenelon

In its history, the United States has been in fourteen
major wars and dozens of minor military skirmishes. World
War II nearly pushed the country to its breaking point, while
the wars in Vietnam and Iraq left not only thousands of casualties, but deep emotional wounds, the kind of wounds that
last for decades, sometimes lifetimes.

All of these wars were horrific, but none of them left
as deep a scar as our own civil war. Not only were there more
deaths—over three-quarters of a million citizens—but it
pitted brother against brother, neighbor against neighbor. It
was a bloody, obscene war, made all the worse by the reality
of fighting fellow countrymen.

The Liberian civil war was no different. Liberians
took up guns and machetes against each other, tribe against
tribe, village against village. Any sense that the government would protect you was dashed by a realization that the
government soldiers had become increasingly lawless and

greedy, making it impossible for anyone to feel safe around either side of the conflict. In fact, the presence of a government soldier meant your life was in even greater jeopardy. There was no relief in seeing them roll into your neighborhood. They were not there to help you. They were there to take your possessions—and maybe your life.

But the rebel soldiers were, in many ways, even more terrifying. Their appearance and actions were far more bizarre and horrifying. Some of them wore wedding dresses in battle. Others wore wigs and masks. They dressed in whatever odd clothes they found in the houses they looted, having overrun whole villages and neighborhoods like swarms of locust. They drove around in cars decorated with the skulls of the people they had killed. Their goal was to terrify people—and it worked. The sight of these rebels struck fear in the hearts of anyone who saw them because their brutality was unmatched.

One notable figure in the conflict was Joshua Blahyi, who went by the name General Butt Naked. During the first Liberian Civil War, Blahyi was said to have led his troops naked, wearing only shoes and carrying only a gun, believing his nakedness protected him from bullets. He later claimed he would sacrifice a victim before each battle. He openly confessed to participating in multiple human sacrifices.

Blahyi's unit was made up of many child soldiers who had been conscripted into battle. He claimed that he and his soldiers, some of them younger than teenagers, killed 20,000 during the conflict. These kids, seemingly heartless and callous, were often under the influence of drugs and many of them were addicts who would do anything for their next fix. They were deeply loyal to Blahyi, willing to do whatever he ordered them to do. So they killed and maimed and terrorized without apparent conscience.

These young rebels were terrifying, but it was the government soldiers who were ransacking and looting the homes of civilians throughout the city. The war presented them the opportunity to get rich through looting. They wore traditional uniforms, giving the air of official authority, but they robbed citizens' homes because they knew they were already on the losing side of the battle. Their fate was all but sealed.

As the battles raged, the government forces drew closer and closer to Yu-jay's neighborhood. In the distance, he could hear constant gunfire, not just with small arms, but with high-caliber guns that even from a mile away sounded like they were right beside him. The battles raged night and day. Those who had holed up in the house had to crawl to the bathroom because anyone who stood up risked getting shot by a stray bullet. One afternoon Yu-jay lay on the floor and studied the front window, already pierced with bullet holes. It was almost too strange to take in: his house and his neighborhood in the middle of a war zone. It didn't make sense.

A young pastor named Zinnah was stranded with them in the house, having been cut off from his home by the fighting. He told the group he had a dream in which he foresaw soldiers attacking their home. He told them this a week before it actually happened. In Liberia, dreams are often regarded as prophecies, a glimpse into the future. For some, if you dream it, it's a message of what is to come. A week later, his prophecy came true.

The morning when the soldiers kicked in their front door "was actually the most beautiful day I've seen in the country as a young kid," according to Jared. "The sun was at the right temperature, the wind was right. But you didn't see any birds, you didn't

Learn More

see any animals. It was just this eerie quietness. When the gunshots stopped, it was just eerie and quiet. To the point where you really didn't want to move, but you had to because it was the only time you would get to move in that whole entire day."

A few mornings later when the soldiers came to loot

the neighborhood, they kicked open their front door and screamed at everyone to get up and go outside immediately. Rosetta couldn't walk because of her ruined foot. She also had a broken collarbone on her left side and horrible bed sores from lying down for so long, barely able to move. The government soldiers came in and saw her mangled foot and immediately accused her of being a rebel soldier.

"That is why you have a broken foot," one said suspiciously, then he kicked her foot hard with his boot, sending shooting pain through her entire body.

"The pain that I was in…" she said, her voice trailing off. "My foot was just hanging there. It's just indescribable. The pain—and the fear."

Despite her evident agony, they pushed Rosetta, along with the rest of the family and the others seeking shelter in the house—a number that had risen to 21 who had been hiding in the home—outside into the front yard. She hobbled out and lined up. When

Learn More

they got outside, she realized in horror something so awful she couldn't fathom it. The soldiers had set their neighbors' house on fire while the family was still trapped inside, killing all of them.

The panic set in and those lined up before the feral

soldiers said their last prayers, certain they, too, were about to die. The soldiers were desperate men on the losing side of a war, facing near certain death themselves. They had nothing to lose. Killing innocent civilians meant nothing to them.

"These soldiers did not care," Yu-jay said. "They could have wasted us and shot us like we were roaches."

As Yu-jay and the others prepared themselves for what was to come, gunshots rang out in the distance. The

Learn More

soldiers stopped in their tracks. Their eyes darted with fear and desperation. They had to get away. Shooting these people now only meant extra time, time they didn't have. They had already ransacked the house, scooping up all the jewelry and money they could find.

Lord, if that is all the ransom I have to pay, that is nothing, Rosetta thought to herself, referring to everything she owned in the world.

The gunfire spooked the soldiers badly enough they allowed the frightened group back in the house, but not before warning them they planned to return and finish the job. All twenty-one of them ran back into the house and got low to the ground. The fighting raged for more than three hours. After the last round of gunfire, there was a ghostly silence. Finally, one man lifted his head and looked out of the front window.

"They are all gone," the man said.

Slowly, they all got up and went outside. They saw bodies everywhere. All of the men who had almost executed them now lay dead on the ground themselves some 50-60 yards away from their home.

When there was no sign of any living soldiers in the neighborhood, Yu-jay and the others ran as fast as they could to one of the houses that seemed safe. The man who lived there had two wives and four kids and his house had miraculously been untouched in the raid. The large group begged to move in with the man because they were so afraid other soldiers would now return to their house. They explained that Rosetta's nice house would attract rebel soldiers assuming the residents were wealthy or worked for the government and they would be targeted for death yet again. The man relented and allowed them to come in and stay. They remained there, still shaken and terrified, for about three days after the raid.

Zinnah, the pastor who had dreamed of the attack on their home had actually left days before the raid in a desperate attempt to find his fiancée. He escaped the attack, but they found out later he never made it to her. Government soldiers had gunned him down.

7

THE DANGEROUS ROAD

"A person often meets his destiny on the road he took to avoid it."
- Jean de La Fontaine

The entire group reeled from what they had just experienced. What was happening to them was beyond all comprehension. Just days earlier everything seemed normal; now they were running for their lives. Half of the group thought they should leave town immediately; the other half didn't believe they could make a trip on foot with Rosetta. Her broken foot and collarbone would make it nearly impossible for her to travel. Ultimately, the scared group decided they had no other choice but to get out right away. Leaving would be difficult, but to stay there would mean facing near-certain death. They had no food and no water and the city was increasingly volatile and unstable with gunfire ringing out through the night.

At nightfall, all of them, including Rosetta, whose leg cast had been removed by the men who took turns cutting it using a surgical blade, ventured out along a two-mile path. They walked together, with Rosetta being carried on the back of her dear Uncle Edwin, watchful against threats that could come at any time, from any direction. They walked along the side of the road past buildings and houses, yet there was no sign of life in any of them. What used to be people's homes were now empty, still, lifeless. There wasn't even the sound of dogs barking or birds chirping. Just an unnatural quiet. Occasionally they would see dead bodies lying around, shot, bloated in the sun.

After walking for many miles, they came upon a group of rebel soldiers who stopped them before they could get too close, pointing guns at them, demanding to know who they were.

"We are not involved in this," someone in their group said, referring to the conflict. "We are just trying to get to a safe place."

"It's not safe for you here," one of the soldiers yelled. "Go back!"

"But we have no food and water," came the reply. "We need to keep going."

The soldiers scowled and began to fire their machine guns at the ground in front of the huddled group. They clearly weren't intending to shoot the civilians—if so, they wouldn't have missed—but they wanted to scare the group into retreating.

It worked. The group hurriedly turned around and headed back home. But the house offered no real refuge. It was still in the middle of an active war zone and there was no way to get food or clean water.

Elsewhere in the heart of the country, Uncle Moses had been enlisted to train the rebels when they found out he was an expert in Tae Kwon Do. He would soon become a valuable asset for them, lending them his expertise in martial arts. He became part of Charles Taylor's security detail and did some training with the rebels. He was a bodyguard and instructor, but never a fighting rebel soldier. During this time, he ran into two of Rosetta's sisters who told him the family was still at the house in the middle of active fighting.

Moses spoke with Taylor directly for permission to have some men, a vehicle, and clearance to travel to Monrovia and pick up the family in the Paynesville area where they lived. Taylor gave his consent and Moses instantly sprang into action. Along with a small group of men, he hopped in a van and drove to the house, having already acquired the cachet to allow him past the checkpoints and into the neighborhood. He found the family, scared and famished.

"We have to get you out," he said and loaded them into the truck with only the personal belongings they could carry by hand. All that Rosetta had worked for—the house, the furnishings, the possessions—were left behind, never to be seen again. At that point, none of them cared. All they wanted was to survive.

"Because life is more than stuff," Rosetta said years later. "And you don't realize that until you're faced with life and death. Then you realize all these things we think make us feel important, are not that important. Life is really what is important."

Moses came at just the right moment to take them away, appearing seemingly out of thin air in a white van with rebel soldiers hanging off the side of it. He hurried the boys along and they quickly hopped in the van and left Monrovia with only the clothes on their backs. Jared wore a pair of Yu-jay's Adidas shoes because he always liked them. Yu-jay grabbed dress shoes and wore them with his shorts. In the weeks to come, he would walk so much he actually wore the heels off of them.

Before they left, they invited the neighbor that had taken them in to leave with them and bring his entire family, but he refused to go. He decided to stay in town and take his chances. Later, they would find out that other soldiers came through the neighborhood and killed the man. Had Yu-jay, Jared, Rosetta, and the rest of them stayed there for even a few more days, they would have surely lost their lives.

Despite the presence of the fierce-looking warriors that surrounded Moses, the boys felt a sense of safety for the first time in days.

"I didn't have any fear at that time," Jared said. "Moses had control over these guys and he was running the show."

They were hopeful they would finally be able to get out of town alive. Moses was delivering them from their oppression and they trusted he would get them to a promised land, a place where they could be safe and restart their lives. But getting out, even with their new deliverer, would not be easy. Fighting encircled them and anyone who stumbled into the wrong territory, no matter who they were, risked losing their lives.

Moses decided to take them to Gbarnga, a town about 122 miles to the northeast of Monrovia and home to around 34,000 residents. It had become the rebel base, the home of Charles Taylor's National Patriotic Front of Liberia. Ironically, since the war, it had become safer to be in that town behind the rebel lines than to be in places where the rebels had yet to advance. Since the rebels were dominating the government forces, the chances of that town being overrun were slim.

Normally it might take about four hours to drive to

Gbargna but with the checkpoints and skirmishes, they all knew it would take much longer. The road there would be treacherous, but no one knew exactly how bad it would be. Moses loaded the boys onto the van and headed out of town.

Several miles down the road, just on the outskirts of town, rebels stopped the van at a makeshift checkpoint looking for government officials who might be trying to flee the city. They didn't have list of names or pictures, so their scrutiny was based far more on guesswork and intuition than any systematic procedure. The soldiers boarded the van and a man who was sitting on board attracted their attention. The man looked well fed and healthy, especially for someone in the middle of a war. They yanked him off the van, accusing him of being part of the Liberian government.

Moses rose up to challenge them. "This guy is okay. I know this guy!" he yelled to the armed men.

In some circles, Moses' word would have been as good as gold, but the soldiers in this more remote area didn't know him and had no intention of listening to him. They marched the terrified man off into the bush, about 50 yards or so. Yujay heard the man protest loudly and scream, then a burst of gunfire from an automatic weapon rang out and the soldiers returned to the road, leaving the dead man in the bush behind them.

"We were on our way to some sort of better life. They took this guy and shot him. We didn't see it, but we heard it," Yu-jay said. "It was like a horror show."

As terrifying as it was to experience this man being killed, it was even more chilling to realize  the rebels had done it just because they had a hunch about the man and the power to do as they pleased, even killing inno-

Learn More cent people just because you didn't like the look of them. They realized all of them could be in jeopardy, even with Moses there to protect them. At the next check-point or road block, any of them could be pulled off the van, marched a few yards into the bush, and executed.

There were more checkpoints to come, but each time, Moses stepped up and worked things out. When they were stopped, Moses would get off the van and speak with the soldiers and smooth out whatever problem the rebels had cooked up, usually to shake them down for money. Rosetta had scraped together some cash before they left, so Moses was able to offer bribes that allowed them to pass until the next roadblock where it all happened again.

They drove through the night and into the next day as their four-hour trip stretched on for over a day. They were repeatedly stopped and Moses had to talk or bribe their way

past one set of soldiers after another. In U.S. dollars, a sat-
isfactory bribe would range from $20 to $100, which quickly
added up. If they hit too many checkpoints, they would be
depleted of cash and turned back.

"This was war," Yu-jay explained. "So the trip was
not a straight shot. It's not like you get in the car, fill up the
tank, and bring a sandwich along."

Once when they were stopped on a bridge, Yu-jay got
out and walked along the edge of the overpass and looked
down into the water below. He saw a terrifying sight: bodies
floating down the river. These black people had been dead
long enough to have their skin bleached in the sun, so they
looked white and puffed up, in different stages of decomposi-
tion.

"I can see it now," he recalled many years later. "The
water running—it was during the day and these bodies obviously had been dead a while. You look at it and you never
forget it. It was pretty scary."

They arrived at the Cotton Tree Gate, unaware that
this would become a notorious checkpoint where the rebel
soldiers killed countless numbers of people, both government
soldiers and civilians alike.

A young woman approached the van. She was one of
the rebel leaders in the area and she ordered them to get out

and give her the van. She wanted the van to get to Buchanan. Moses argued forcefully with her, but she would not back down. She was determined to take their van. Moses came up with a compromise: he would travel with her to Buchanan, then return with the van as soon as he could. He told the group he had no other choice if they had any hope of keeping the van. He promised to return as soon as he was able to, then got in the van with the young woman and took off, leaving the rest of them to figure out what to do next. They would not see Uncle Moses again for several weeks.

The group decided to head out toward Bong Mines, a mining community that was rumored to be peaceful even now in the midst of the war. Rosetta's close friends, Becky and Jaye, lived in Bong Mines and had hosted the boys for vacation often when they were not in school. They knew the town fairly well, having visited there many times over the years. They asked the driver of a huge dirt dump truck for a ride. He told them he could take them as far as a town named Kakata—if they were willing to ride in the back. They took what they could get and loaded themselves into the rear of the giant dump truck. Even Rosetta had to get in the back of the truck with her broken collarbone and crushed ankle with no place she could lie down comfortably.

"There was no room in the truck. You couldn't move,"

Jared said. "If your head was down, it would be down for hours."

The driver dropped them off in the village just before Kataka. A woman who was with the rebel faction there saw them and was sympathetic to their plight, especially after observing Rosetta's deeply diminished state, so she took them into her house for the evening. They were able to get a meal and a decent night sleep.

The next day, they set out on foot to Kakata, which was only a few miles away. That relatively short distance proved to be one of the most dangerous legs of the entire trip.

"Everything was crazy. You would see people getting harassed, people getting beat," Jared recalled. "You would see people walking down the street with guns saying crazy stuff and you just walk and hope that nobody talks to you. You don't want to have any eye contact. You just hope that you can just keep walking."

At last, they arrived in Kakata and actually saw some people they knew. It was a huge relief. The town felt much safer than anything else they had experienced on the trip so far. They waited a long time for a bus headed toward Bong Mines and they were exhausted, but they didn't mind the wait. At least they felt safe for the time being.

The bus ride to Bong Mines was mercifully uneventful

and they arrived in the town with no other major scares or roadblocks. A German-operated company ran the little town and its employees were still mining every day, giving the community a much more stable feel than the surrounding areas.

"No matter how many people were getting killed or what war was going on, the factories and farms continued to make products. Companies still made profits even in wartime," Jared said.

The mining town was also nearly behind rebel lines, so there was not as much fighting and gunfire. Despite all this, there were still menacing soldiers roaming around and rumors of indiscriminate killings.

To their delight, they would find safe shelter in Bong Mines with Becky and Jaye. The couple had a nice home located in a beautiful neighborhood on a golf course with a community pool. They even had 24-hour television, which in those days in Liberia, was remarkable. It was Yu-jay and his family's favorite vacation destination when school closed. Jaye worked in employee relations for the large German iron ore mining company. He served as a liaison between the German management team and Liberian employees and government. But the situation even this town was not the safest place to be. Rebel soldiers could still do whatever they wanted with impunity. Their host family had to bargain with the rebels for food, which had become scarce, as supply lines became cut off. Rosetta's broken body from the accident was still in severe pain. Her right ankle was especially in need of urgent medical attention. It had become infected and looked dead, probably in need of amputation. If she had any hope of saving her foot, she had to get out of the country.

A week after arriving in Bong Mines, a friend urged her to go to Ivory Coast where there would be a working hospital that could take care of her foot. Rosetta felt her heart sink. She had left everything she had in her old house and now she only had $100 to her name. The chance of getting out of the country and finding real medical care with only $100 was very low.

Just weeks earlier, the thought of losing all that they owned would have been unbelievable and devastating. She had overcome so much and worked very hard to acquire all she had. Now, this huge loss was almost an afterthought.

"We didn't care," she explained of losing all of her earthly possessions and her house. "When there is life and death, you don't care about anything except life. That was it. So we didn't care about what we lost or what we had."

She decided to risk the trip. It was the only chance she had, even though the chances of getting to Ivory Coast were desperately low. She knew she had to go without her boys because the chance of her dying on the road was high and she couldn't bear to take her children into that uncertainty. She couldn't stand the thought of her children watching her die, or worse yet, watching them die or be killed on the road with her.

"If I go, I prefer to die alone than for my children to die with me," she explained.

She asked her friend, Becky, to watch after her boys and her mother while she tried to make her way to Ivory Coast for medical attention. She gathered her family together one last time before she left.

Learn More

"I was going into the unknown," she said later. "And I said, 'If you don't hear from me, that means I didn't make it.' And I cried and kissed them goodbye."

After she left for Ivory Coast with another couple she had been close with in Monrovia, the boys stayed with Becky and Jaye in Bong Mines and enjoyed some level of normalcy—especially playing with friends and being able to sleep through the night without the constant sounds of war to frighten them. But staying long term was not a viable option. Food was in short supply as the town became increasingly unstable and unsafe. A few weeks after they had arrived at Becky and Jaye's home in Bong Mines, the couple decided to take everyone to Gbargna, the town where Moses had planned to bring them in the first place. Gbarnga was a several hours away. They would take a public bus, like an American Greyhound bus, that would make several stops on the way. Scraping what little money they had, Becky and Jaye would purchase seats for their family and Yu-jay and Jared as they traveled to get further away from active fighting, not toward it. There was safety ahead—or so they thought.

8

BEHIND ENEMY LINES

"Man's enemies are not demons, but human beings like himself."
- Lao Tzu

One of the more famous residents of Gbarnga is Tamba Hali, an NFL linebacker for the Kansas City Chiefs. The future Pro Bowler came to the United States to become a highly successful professional athlete.[1] Yu-jay and Tamba were only seven years apart in age and probably never met while they were both living in this small town, but they were faced with the same reality of being kids who saw their home country crumbling around them. Tamba and his family ended up fleeing the country four years later.

Yu-jay, Jared, along with Jaye and Becky's family and others who had traveled with them from Monrovia arrived in Tamba's hometown unharmed, but they saw many casualties of the war along the way and even in town. It was apparent to them that the battles in the area had been fierce until the rebels took control of the town. The current calm stood in contrast to what this town had experienced just weeks before.

When the war came, Jaye and Becky lost nearly everything they owned, just like most everyone else. They did, however, have access to a family house in this remote town of Gbarnga. The house would be their new home and a place they hoped to ride out the war.

Over time, Yu-jay managed to get himself into the daily routine of the new home, but still felt incredibly unsettled most of the time, especially in the evening. He was unfamiliar with the house and the grounds at night. The property became incredibly dark in the evening since it was cut off from the power grid and there were no outdoor lights, except for the moon and stars. Yu-jay would make his way around the property in the pitch black using only a small flashlight with a dim bulb. The feeling that anyone hiding in the darkness could jump or stab him filled him with a deep sense of dread. It was a hard feeling to shake when you had just fled your own home under cover of darkness for fear of being killed without warning.

As Yu-jay was feeling emotionally shaky, Jared began to feel physically shaky. It was clear he had contracted jaundice, which, if untreated, can cause liver failure. He needed to get to the nearest operating hospital right away. The good news was that one of the

Learn More

largest hospitals in the country outside of Monrovia was in the area; the bad news is that it was several miles away. At first, he tried to hitch a ride, but no one would take him. After that failed, two of the older boys in the house agreed to walk with him, but when they realized how lengthy the trek was, they turned back, leaving him to get there on his own.

When he arrived, there were no open rooms in the entire hospital because they were all full of people who had been shot and wounded during the armed conflict in town and in the surrounding area. They attempted to treat him in the emergency room. A nurse gave him a shot of penicillin, despite the fact that he was allergic to it, and sent him on his way. The injection left him dizzy and disoriented. He staggered back to the house, somehow making it all the way home by himself.

"They always used to think that I was not afraid because I was good at showing no emotions," Jared said. "Now because of my experience, I'm really not afraid of anything."

He recovered but he found himself getting sick nearly every time he traveled. His foot got badly infected on one occasion and he wasn't able to walk for a while. He got malaria on multiple other occasions. Despite all this, Jared was still considered the physically stronger of the two brothers. He was sent away during the daytime hours to work on a farm, which was risky in the open, remote areas that were crawling with soldiers and buzzing with bullets that sometimes whizzed overhead.

Eventually Yu-jay and Jared ended up being sent about two miles away to another house because Jay and Becky's house became so crowded with other family members of theirs who were seeking refuge from the fighting in the city. They made friends with the other kids in the area, many of them child soldiers. When these young soldiers were off-duty, Yu-jay and Jared would hang out with them and play soccer and Scrabble and other board games. The kids who had been conscripted to fight seemed normal most of the time, but most of them would have a lifetime of emotional scars from being forced into war as children.

One day when Yu-jay was playing outside with another boy, a rebel soldier passing by stopped and sized him up.

"This boy will make a good child soldier," the man said. He walked up to Yu-jay and looked him in the eye. "I'll come back and get you tomorrow."

Learn More

A jolt of terror shot through Yu-jay. He and the other boy ran off and told Jaye and Becky what the soldier had said. The couple hid him in another friend's house. For more than a day, Yu-jay laid low, trying desperately to avoid being grabbed by the man and conscripted as a child soldier.

"The worst thing you could be was a child soldier," Yu-jay said. He already knew what fate would await him if he were to be conscripted. It would be a life of violence and substance abuse and emotional wreckage. He knew if the man grabbed him, the course of his life would be dramatically different.

"They had kids as young as seven or so who were child soldiers," Yu-jay explained. "Those kids who are child soldiers are ruined for life. They were doing things you can't even imagine when they should have been playing with toys."

The man never did find Yu-jay and no other soldiers came looking for him, but that didn't mean he was out of danger, even in the relative safety of Gbarnga. His greatest threat actually took place at the hands of a child younger smaller than him in body size. Yu-jay had small scars on his wrists that looked like tally marks. They had been placed there near the time of his birth out of superstition. Children in Liberia and other West African countries were often given marks on their hands or arms or even on their faces that were supposed to protect them from evil spirits. However, during the war, a faction of the rebels that had broken away from Charles Taylor to follow Prince Johnson had distinguished themselves by cutting a series of six marks on their forearms. The smaller kid, a child soldier, saw the marks on Yu-jay's arm and pointed his gun at him.

"You're the enemy," he said to Yu-jay.

"No!" Yu-jay protested, but the boy would not be reasoned with. He ordered Yu-jay to stand up and the boy began to walking him into the woods to execute him. Yu-jay's cousin was with him on this day and became frantic, trying to get the smaller boy to stop, but it was clear the kid was determined to shoot Yu-jay for his perceived treason.

"This kid had a gun—a small kid with a gun! These kids were just the most vicious rebel soldiers because they almost did things without a real sense of what they were doing. That was crazy, someone saying they were going to kill you," Yu-jay said. He knew the boy was not bluffing. He truly intended to shoot Yu-jay.

As they marched into the woods, the scene became surreal. While his cousin pleaded with the armed boy to stop, Yu-jay flashed back to the scene on the van that had happened only a few weeks earlier where the man suspected of being a government official was dragged off the bus and into the bush where he was shot dead. He knew the same thing could easily happen to him and all at the hands of this little boy who had no concept of life and death. The boy was so little Yu-jay could have taken him in a fair fight, but now the kid had a gun pointed at the back of his head.

They came across a couple of adult soldiers who stopped the kid in his tracks and asked him to explain what was happening. The boy showed the marks on Yu-jay's wrist, certain they were evidence of his involvement with the renegade faction. Yu-jay pleaded with the men, reasoning with them. The younger boy shouted over him.

"No, no, no! Those are not the same marks," one of the soldiers said. "Cool your jets, little man." They ordered the kid to release Yu-jay, which he did with a disappointed scowl.

Had they not been there on that day, the little boy would have undoubtedly killed Yu-jay in the bush. This was the insanity of the war. You could be murdered by anyone, even a young child. It was lawlessness, even in a seemingly peaceful town.

Weeks later, Yu-jay recalled seeing the boy walked down a neighborhood path in a carefree way. Rage ran through Yu-jay in a way he had never experienced before.

"I've never in my entire life thought about killing somebody, but I'll never forget I just thought about running him down and hitting him in the head with a rock or something. That was probably the most violent thought I've had in my life," Yu-jay said. "I will never forget that because I had that thought: 'I want to hurt this person.' And he was just walking around like any other little kid. I just recall that emotion and it was so strong that I will never forget it."

---

[1] Tamba Hali is also known for his generosity, having once left a $1300 tip at a restaurant and helping fund the construction of an Ebola clinic in his home country during the 2014 outbreak.

9

WEARY JOURNEYS

"Oh, I am very weary
Though tears no longer flow
My eyes are tired of weeping
My heart is sick of woe."
- Anne Brontë

Rosetta had set off for Ivory Coast with a friend and her husband, desperately hoping she would find medical attention in time to save her foot. The trip was a descent into darkness. At nearly every turn, they saw murderous rebel soldiers, crazed with power, intimidating and frightening innocent people. The rebels would use their guns to push people around and scare them. On one occasion, they witnessed the rebels tying up a man and stuffing him into a large rice sack. They tied it shut and tossed the bound man into the river, where he died in a watery grave. These kinds of atrocities were commonplace now. Human life appeared to have little value.

"On our way, they were executing people," she said. "They were tying them up and butchering them."

The trip to Ivory Coast was slow and treacherous. On any normal day before the war ripped through the country, it would have taken only a couple of hours to get to the border, but during the madness of the civil conflict, it took them much longer because of the constant checkpoints and stoppages. The trip seemed like it would never end.

At long last, Rosetta, her friend and her husband, and a busload of others fleeing the war, made it to the border and were able to enter the Ivory Coast. Once safely inside the boundaries of the new country, they had their first full meal in many weeks in the home of a couple named the Witherspoons, another one of Rosetta's old friends from back home in Monrovia. They were all emaciated and starving. Rosetta was so weakened from trauma and starvation that her hand trembled as she ate that first piece of meat and that first egg. Despite being so hungry, she could only eat a few bites because it felt as if her stomach had shrunk.

Rosetta was able to get to an adequate hospital in Abidjan and receive proper care and treatment for her badly injured foot. The medical staff set her badly shattered right ankle and placed it in a cast. For the first time in days, she felt some respite from the throbbing, stabbing pain in her foot. She also felt some emotional relief, not constantly having to fear for her life.

"Just not to hear gunshots every minute, I just couldn't even imagine," she said.

The emotional respite and the relief of finally getting treatment for her foot were soon matched by the grief of being separated from her boys. When her pain finally subsided and the nights were quiet, the awful reality of her family's situation set in and it filled her with an incredible sadness. As she lay in recovery, she resolved to get her children back as soon as she was able.

To do that, she first needed to heal, but then she would need cash to pay for travel and bribes along the way.

Before she had any idea her life was going to be upended, Rosetta had already secured and paid for a visa to travel to the U.S. Once there, she intended to sell her lapas, dried shrimp and fish, and other Liberian goods that were big sellers among the expatriates there. The option of selling anything in America had disappeared when she left her house and all her earthly possessions behind, but the chance to go to the U.S. might open up more opportunities for her to get her boys. There were more connections, more money, and more influence there. She knew that heading to the States, where she had visited a few times in the past, was her best move when her body would allow. Fortunately, members from the church she attended in Abidjan, along with several Liberians who lived in the country, pooled their money to help her purchase a ticket to the US where she could receive additional treatment for her broken ankle and clavicles.

Back in Gbarnga, conditions were beginning to deteriorate as the war became more intense. The city became increasingly unsafe. Charles Taylor was in constant fear of being assassinated and would wear full body armor and travel with an entourage of bodyguards, even in this town that was considered rebel territory. The idea that there might possibly be secret agents or undercover operatives in their midst set the whole town on edge and added to the sense of instability. The possibility of Yu-jay becoming conscripted as a child soldier or having another unhinged kid hurt or kill him, along with the dwindling food supplies, pushed the group along to another more remote location, a place where there were fewer soldiers and less fighting. They chose to go to a village deep in the bush called Voloblai. They would have to walk again. This time, it would be 20 miles by foot.

The adults expected Yu-jay to fall apart on the approximately 8-hour foot trek to Voloblai because he was an asthmatic, seemingly weak kid. He was viewed as a sickly mama's boy, while his brother Jared was strong and fit. Much to everyone's surprise, though, he held up better than most of the others. In fact, he never seemed to get sick during the time of war. Ironically, it was Jared who ended up getting seriously ill during this time.

They traveled with a cousin named Augustine who was nicknamed LPC, short for "Liberian Professional Coach," a common soccer term. LPC was impressed with Yu-jay's toughness for the journey.

"My cousin, LPC, told me that I showed some real toughness doing that," Yu-jay said, referring to the arduous trip. The refugee experience had already begun to create real mental and physical resilience in him.

Once they arrived at Voloblai, they found there was not a lot to eat in the village, so they were forced to hunt and farm for their own food. Any kind of food was a luxury, but the village community tended to share what they had. Often scraps or pieces of meat would be put into a large bowl and the kids would gather around it and eat together, using their hands to tear pieces and scoop up bites. The other boys from the village were incredibly fast. By the time Yu-jay had eaten a single scoop, these boys had already downed 9 or 10 handfuls. The boys had rough hands from their years of tough labor in the bush. They could carry hot charcoal with their bare hands or rip into a side of beef with blazing speed. Yu-jay was a city boy with soft hands who moved much slower than the well-practiced local kids. He was certain to get the least amount of food of any of the boys in the circle. To compensate, he began carrying a small spoon around in his pocket that he had salvaged from his stay in Gbarnga.

"I was annoyed that I couldn't keep up," he said. "So my spoon was my way of survival. I can eat fast with a spoon. I eventually got better at it."

Hunger was a daily, almost moment-to-moment, experience for Yu-jay and the others in the tiny village. One day, Yu-jay and some of the boys were out in the bush exploring when they came upon an orange orchard, still full of fresh, healthy oranges.

Learn More

"The rules were that you could eat as many oranges as you wanted, but you had to keep the seeds and peels together because it was a functioning farm," Jared explained.

They were so hungry, they just ate orange after orange. He estimated they ate 10 or 12 oranges each. As delicious and filling as it was, the fruit's citric acid wreaked havoc on their guts and they paid the price for their indulgence well into the night.

But hunger was not the only threat in Voloblai. From time to time, rebel soldiers would arrive without notice and walk through town, even in this remote, isolated little village. Fear seized the residents when the rebels showed up.

"In the bush, they could kill a whole town and no one

would ever know," Yu-jay explained. "You're always at the mercy of the soldiers."

Despite this, the soldiers didn't cause trouble for the people of Voloblai, at least during the time when Yu-jay and Jared were there. The last time they came through when the brothers were there, a handful of tough-looking guys swept through the town inspecting the place, eyeing the people, but they left without incident and without looting.

As before, Yu-jay and Jared settled into the rhythm of village life. They explored and played and hung out with the other boys. One day, Yu-jay and some other boys were out at a swimming hole and he dove headfirst, unaware of how shallow the water was.

A jarring thud shook his entire body.

He had split his head open on a rock. Stunned and rattled by the impact and the pain, he stood up in the water. His face was covered with blood. It spooked the children so badly they all turned and ran away from him. The injury would prove to be minor but it served as a picture of the emotional experience of the previous few months where at any time, even the most tranquil and peaceful of days could bring unexpected danger, bloodiness, even death. The whole country was traumatized, on high alert all the time.

Yu-jay and Jared were put to work in the village,

often having to carry bags of seed that weighed 60 or even as much as 80 pounds, which was more than Yu-jay weighed at the time. To transport the bags, they would have to carry them in their arms or on their heads across the river. Several times Yu-jay would get leeches on him. As he emerged from the water, the leeches would be all over his legs. The older men would take a knife and cut them off of him, with the risk that they might take some of his own skin off with it.

"That was crazy, having leeches on me," he said. "You don't want that ever. Not fun."

The boys spent about a month in Voloblai and things were not much better. Soldiers still swarmed. The drums

Learn More

of war were beating. They needed to get out. Once again, Moses returned at just the right moment to retrieve them. He brought them back to Gbarnga for a week or so to get their documents in order so they could get over the border. Moses worked his charm and bribed a border guard into giving them Laissez-pass-ers, which were travel documents that they believed would allow the boys to cross into Ivory Coast and be reunited with their mother. By this time, Rosetta had recovered sufficiently enough to be able to fly out of Ivory Coast to the United States. She intended to return for the boys and bring them back to the U.S. She had arrived there safely and was able to send Moses enough money to get the boys over the border.

"If you don't have the money, you can't get out of the country," Jared said.

They set out to cross the border, but there was no guarantee they would make it across. Getting out of Liberia could mean the difference between life and death for all of them.

10

THE BORDER

"A hero is somebody who voluntarily walks into the unknown."
- Tom Hanks

The day the border passes arrived, Jared came down with symptoms of malaria, which included high fever, shaking chills, sweating, headache, and nausea. Despite his illness, he loaded up on a truck with Moses and Yu-jay, and they drove out under cover of darkness and pushed deep into Nimba County, a rural area known not just for mining, but for its eeriness. It was a remote land, largely cut off from the larger towns and notorious for superstition and stories of supernatural events, like witches who transformed into jungle cats or dragons. Even decades later during the 2014 Ebola outbreak, a story from Nimba County that three people who had been confirmed to have died of the disease had come back to life as "Ebola Zombies" spread like wildfire, sending news crews into the bush to investigate the claim. The story was ultimately discredited as a hoax, of course, but it underscored how readily such tales are given credibility in the region. Even a casual visit to Nimba County often leaves one with an ominous feeling that anything could happen. Jared called the trip into the remote area "terrifying." They could be attacked by rogues and no one could stop them. Even worse, they could be grabbed by heartmen, witch doctors who kidnap people and cut out their hearts while they are still alive and use them to make potions and medicine. Apparently tales of the heartmen were partially based on truth.

In her excellent book , The House at Sugar Beach, Helene Cooper, a Liberian-born American journalist who works as a Pentagon correspondent for the New York Times, gives a harrowing account of a boy being chased down the beach by a heartman wielding a machete. The boy escaped, but had he not, he would have been murdered on the coastline and his body would have been dragged away, never to be seen again.

The superstitions and the fearfulness were rooted in tradition that went back generations, but were intensified by the reign of Samuel Doe. He allegedly had massacred over 300 people in the region following the infamous "Nimba Raid" of 1983. In that raid, a group of men from an ethnic clan in the region attacked the house of a prominent geologist in the mining town. In response, Doe ordered hundreds of men, women, and children arrested. They were reportedly lined up and shot, then dumped in a mass grave. Two years later, after a failed coup against him, Doe is alleged to have set up a death squad that rounded up and executed many of the citizens of Nimba County.

At that time, travelers through the region would be asked what language they spoke or what tribe they were from or what their last name was. If they didn't like your answer, you were as good as dead. They would go as far as checking the imprints a person's socks pressed against their legs. Government soldiers had to wear rubber bands to keep their socks up, leaving an indentation. If Nimba soldiers saw that impression on your leg, you would be shot. They also looked for scars that might identify you as being from another tribe.

Yu-jay and Jared were on a truck that had no other choice but to drive through the middle of this hostile, superstitious, and violent land to get to where they needed to go. As they drove through the pitch-black jungle road, an animal of some sort—Jared and Yu-jay never saw it—darted in front of them in a flash and was struck and killed by the truck. The driver got out and skinned and cooked the animal for the starving group. But the man chose to feed only himself and his own people and leave Yu-jay and Jared hungry. In desperate times, people often reveal their true character. Some, like Moses, make sacrifices for others, while many, like the driver, eat and leave the children to go hungry.

On well-paved roads, the trip would have taken no longer than four hours, but in this remote land, the dirt paths, full of mud holes and mounds took between seven and eight hours. There was a large refugee camp just over the border in a town called Danané. Later, it would be said that the majority of all Liberians who fled the civil war and came to the United States ended up in the refugee camp in Danané at some point during their journey. If they could reach the camp, they would be out of their war-torn home country and in the relative safety of Ivory Coast.

However, when they finally arrived at the border be-tween Nimba and Ivory Coast, the guards would not allow them to cross into the country. Though the Ivorian government was allowing some refuges into the coun-

Learn More try, many were turned away. Their documents were not in proper order, or so the security officials said. Once again, Moses stepped in. He spoke fluent French and argued with the men until they let them past the checkpoint.

"At each point, he had to argue with someone to get through," Jared recalled.

Moses prevailed and they were finally allowed to pass into the country and reunite with their beloved and very-missed mom, who had been awaiting their arrival after almost six months of separation.

Jared was reeling from the full effects of malaria—the pounding headache, the fever and chills—but there was really no time and no place to be sick. The camp was overflowing with refugees, many crammed into small rooms, sleeping on floors.

"There were a lot of people there. I think we even ran into some people we knew. We slept on the floor with a bunch of people," Yu-jay recalled.

About a week prior to this reunion, Rosetta had arrived on a Sunday in Ivory Coast from the USA without a true plan and no idea where to go or who could help her. Today in Liberia, Ivory Coast, and much of Africa, cell phones are relatively commonplace, but practically no one had access to a cell phone or internet service at  **Learn More** that time. As a result, information was hard to come by and Rosetta was cut off from all avenues to track down her boys. She went to the Liberian Embassy because she knew that was where many of the displaced Liberians gathered to have some semblance of community and support each other.

"They just came together and talked. It was so therapeutic for them," she said.

On her first visit, while the trips to the Embassy and the camaraderie of fellow Liberians who all shared similar stories proved to be replenishing for her, her inability to find anyone with knowledge of her sons' whereabouts was crushing.

By the next morning, her frustration began to shift toward desperation. Her boys were out there somewhere, but she couldn't find them. She could find no one who knew exactly where they were, including the other Liberians who had heard from other relatives back in Liberia. The thought of taking matters into her own hands and venturing into Liberia to search for them on her own entered her mind. But she knew this would be like trying to find two little needles in a giant African haystack. On her second visit to the Embassy, her fortunes changed as she found Moses there, waiting for her, having just arrived from Liberia to check on the boys.

"Isn't that a miracle?" she asked later. "I didn't even know where he was—and there was Moses. He said, 'Sis Rose, I saw the kids last night.'"

"Really?!" she exclaimed. "How did you know I was going to be here?"

"I just felt in my spirit that you were coming," he replied.

Had Moses not shown up, Rosetta had already decided to board the bus herself that evening and make her way to the border, but the idea of going alone was terrifying. It put her near the reach of the rebels once again and she had no idea where the boys might be or how to make contact with them. But Moses once again arrived at the right moment to reunite her with her boys.

When he arrived with them, a few days after she had arrived in the Ivory Coast , Rosetta caught a glimpse of her boys stepping off the bus. It was like a shock of electricity.

"I couldn't talk. They couldn't talk," she said, refer-ring to seeing each other the first time in months. "When they got out of that bus, I remember seeing Tiney (Jared's nickname) coming first and then Yu-jay. And I just held them for a long time. I cried and I couldn't sleep that night."

Learn More

They stayed up late and the boys told her of what they had experienced: the traumas and the near-misses, the times when Moses came at just the right time to intervene, the families that had taken them in and cared for them.

"I couldn't even cry," she said. "I used to cry all the time, but I didn't have tears because of all the joy. It was just overwhelming."

11

CLOSE TO NORMAL

"The conventional definition of reality, and the idea of 'normal life', mean nothing."
- Sigmar Polke

Before she left for the U.S., Rosetta had met an Ivorian couple in church who lived in Abidjan, the former capital city of Ivory Coast ("Cote d'Ivoire," as the country calls itself), some 470 miles from Monrovia, far from the conflict in her troubled home country. The couple, who didn't know the family at all, had agreed to take them all in until they could secure passage to the United States. After a few more nights in the refugee camp, Rosetta arranged transportation to the couple's home.

Abidjan is a large and beautiful city of around 4.5 million people, considered by most to be the cultural hub of West African. It is the third largest French-speaking city in the world and the second largest city in all of West Africa. The metropolis sits in the midst of a two-mile wide lagoon on several peninsulas and islands knitted together by a network of bridges. The city has huge stretches of high-rises, stadiums, and office complexes, punctuated by large areas of lush trees and coastal highways. Despite the country's own political and economic hardships over the past several decades, it was then and now a thriving city with universities and banking centers.

When they arrived, the couple took them into their home with open arms and no strings attached.

"It was amazing. It was like a whole new world," Yu-jay said of the city and of the beautiful home where they were now living.

The family had an established routine that felt safe and comforting to the boys. Yu-jay recalled the pattern of everyone going to work or school from 8:00 a.m. until 12:00 noon, then coming home for a few hours for a nap time, then returning from 3:00 p.m. until 5:00 p.m. The siesta time in the middle of the day was a long-standing tradition in the country, likely an influence of the country's tight linkage to France. It created a predictable rhythm to each day.

"It was just beautiful. I loved it," Yu-jay said. "We would go to their house for lunch and sit at this long beautiful table, eating, watching cartoons, especially Teenage Mutant Ninja Turtles in French. It was almost like it marked this sort of transition from a time of war and famine and lacking and fear to this time of plenty and just starting to live life and be kids again. I just really enjoyed that."

Jared agreed. "Living in Abidjan was nice," he re-called. "Things started to become normal."

While they were there, they met Reed Kramer and Tami Hultman, the owners of AllAfrica Global Media in Abidjan. The Kramers would later interview them and write about their story for Africa News, an Africa-focused newsletter they published and distributed to a large audience. Many read the story and it began to draw attention to their personal plight and the dire situation in all of Liberia. The story, in fact, was one of the human-interest articles that began to create greater awareness in the international community of the horrible situation in Liberia.

Both Yu-jay and Jared enjoyed being with the Ivorian couple and especially being back with their mom, but their reunion would be short-lived, however. Rosetta had a round-trip ticket to return to the U.S. Despite her best efforts, she could not get visas for the boys to leave the country with her. Four times she applied for visas; four times she was denied. She kept going back and kept getting turned down, usually for no clear reason. They all believed that Rosetta's good service working for the U.S. government at the U.S. embassy in Monrovia would put her in the good graces of the officials who were responsible of issuing the visas, but the war changed all the rules. Again and again, they were denied.

This meant Rosetta would have to return to the U.S. alone to petition for the visas and the boys would have to return to the refugee camp.

"That was really, really shocking," Yu-jay said, referring to the visa denials. "I don't remember all the back and forth of what happened, but I do remember my mom just sobbing because her plan was to take us with her."

Once again there was a terrible separation, made all the worse because they had been reunited for a while and were living at semblance of a normal life for the first time in months. Still, it had to be done and Rosetta set out once again for the United States and the boys returned to the refugee camp to live with Becky and Jaye. They were so close, but their nightmare was not yet over.

12

SOUTHERN COMFORT

"The most beautiful voice in the world is that of an educated Southern woman."
- Winston Churchill

Mary Ann Taylor can light up a room with her magnetic personality. A woman possessed of uncommon Southern charm and grace, she is beloved by many and has rich relationships that have filled her life across many decades. One friend of hers described her as "a beautiful, sweet, and kind lady." She was also described as "full of energy, easy to talk to, and easy to love." That kindness and ability to love others was also tempered with a tenacity and forcefulness when needed that came in handy when Rosetta's story intersected her own.

When Mary Ann Taylor was four-years-old, she told her mother that she knew what she wanted to do when she grew up.

"What's that?" her mother asked, undoubtedly amused by the precocious conclusion.

"I want to help people," little Mary Ann said.

"How will you do that?" her mother inquired.

"Well, I'll take them flowers to make them feel better."

Years later, at the age of thirteen, her plan to help people gained a little more clarity. This time she knew what she wanted to be. Having just come back from Camp Caswell, a former military base on Oak Island, NC, that had been converted to a retreat center, young Mary Ann had just heard a missionary woman speak over the weekend. Mary Ann announced to her mother that she now wanted to be a missionary.

"Don't ever speak to me about this again!" said her mother with an anger that surprised Mary Ann. Her mother quickly shut down the possibility. Mary Ann was stunned by her mother's negative response, so she didn't bring it up again, but she held onto the hope that someday she would help those overseas.

Later in life when she had married Tom Taylor, the two of them were members of a Sunday School class at First Baptist Church in Charlotte, taught by a man named Tom Bowers, an American who had grown up in Liberia. As Tom spoke of his life in Liberia, Mary Ann became fascinated by his stories of life there. Months later, a Liberian family visited the class, and, once again, her heart was stirred to help people in some far-flung country she didn't know much about. The Taylors befriended the family. Through the friendship, the Taylors would learn more about Liberian culture, as well as the civil war that was tearing up this beautiful country.

One Sunday morning, one of her new Liberian friends introduced her to another Liberian, Mr. Diggs, who worked at a chemical company and taught African Studies at Davidson College. Before coming to the U.S., he had worked in the Liberian Government when William Tubman was the President of Liberia.[1] About a month after their first introduction, Mr. Diggs called and asked Mary Ann for a huge favor. Could she take a Liberian woman who had recently come to America to the doctor? The woman had worked at the American Embassy, he explained to Mary Ann, and she was still suffering pain from the wounds she received during the war.

The woman, of course, was Rosetta. Mary Ann readily agreed and took her to see Dr. Frank Young, a medical missionary who was then stationed in Charlotte. However, after inspecting her foot, Dr. Young said he could not do the surgery she required, which was to remove the steel pins that had been inserted during a procedure at ELWA Hospital in Liberia. He said nothing could be done for her painful collarbone injury either, since it had healed incorrectly. Dr. Young referred Rosetta to an orthopedic doctor for surgery, but Mary Ann found out the cost was going to be exorbitant.

Mary Ann pleaded with Dr. James Pressley, an orthopedic surgeon, to do the surgery at no cost, which he agreed to do.

From that point on, Mary Ann and Rosetta had a tight bond. When she learned of the struggle Rosetta faced obtaining visas for her boys left back in Liberia, she swiftly kicked into the same gear of advocating for her once again. She explored every option of getting Rosetta back to West Africa to retrieve her sons.

She was determined to get airline tickets for Rosetta to return to Ivory Coast and return with Yu-jay and Jared to the United States as soon as possible. Not having the means to purchase the expensive tickets herself—one way tickets ranged in the thousands of dollars—she reached out to an African-based airline. In her letter to the president of Air Afrique Airlines dated January 4, 1991, Mary Ann referred to another shared American-Liberian tragedy, the crash of Pan Am Flight 151 forty years earlier.

On June 22, 1951, Pan Am Flight 151 lost contact with ground control over a remote part of Liberia. An aerial search was unable to locate the missing four-engine plane. Lutheran missionary Louis Bowers dispatched a messenger from the village of Sanoyea. The man brought back bad news the following day: the plane had crashed into the side of a fifteen-hundred foot mountain in a remote area of Liberia.

It was completely disintegrated and there were no apparent survivors among the 31 passengers and 9 crew members.

Jamie Bowers, now the Communications Director for a U.S. Congressman, is the grandson of Rev. Louis Bowers. He writes of the event:

> Search planes had already been unsuccessfully crisscrossing the area for a full day when a messenger brought my grandfather news of the crash site, 17 miles away through rather inaccessible jungle. Having no shortwave radio to relay the news, he immediately dispatched a mission employee to drive the 2 hours to Robertsfield while he stayed behind and attempted to signal the search planes, climbing onto the roof and waving a towel to point pilots in the right direction.

Several of the area missionaries and local tribal people pushed deep into the rugged terrain to reach the site to search for anyone that might possibly by some miracle be found alive. Again, Jamie Bowers writes:

The rescue party included an official from the U.S. Embassy, sent to retrieve a metal briefcase handcuffed to one of the victims. Despite my grandfather warning rescuers that there were no roads, the search team attempted to drive through the jungle before being forced to continue on foot.

When they arrived, they found no signs of life, so they began the sad work of bringing bodies and body parts down from the mountain. It was the rainy season, so they slogged through torrential downpours and waded across flooded areas with water three or more feet deep.

In her 1961 book, Gift From The African Heart, Elizabeth Bowne, a widow of one of the pilots, describes how she visited the remote area nine months later. She found that despite the warnings and threats of the tribal chief, the local people had shown great compassion for the dead, in defiance of superstitions. One tribesman, an elderly deaf man, had carved a huge coffin for the nine crew members and the tribe had buried the dead in a beautiful area with flowers set atop the grave site. They seemed to understand the pain and heartbreak the Americans had experienced with their great loss and they showed great compassion for Elizabeth and other family members.

Jamie Bowers' father was only two years old at the time, but he ended up spending most of childhood in that remote village closest to the crash site. The tragedy and its painful aftermath made a huge impact on the local people and the missionaries for decades to come. The village blacksmith forged an aluminum cross out of some small pieces of metal from the wreckage and gave it to Jamie's father, a physical symbol of the bond they all shared.

Mary Ann's reason for referencing this story in her letter was clear: in the past, both African and American people had shown great compassion during a time of tragedy that affected them all. Now, it was time to do it again. She asked the airline to offer Rosetta a roundtrip ticket to return to Ivory Coast to retrieve her sons.

Despite the impassioned plea, she got no response,[2] but Mary Ann was undeterred. She and her friends raised money for the ticket and got Rosetta back to Africa to be reunited with Yu-jay and Jared.

There was roadblock upon roadblock, obstacle upon obstacle, frustration upon frustration. Nearly every attempt to navigate the situation was met with resistance or apathy or outright hostility. At each point, though, Mary Ann, like Rosetta, pushed as hard as she could. Without political connections or clout, Mary Ann had to resort to sheer persistence and tenacity. When the Consul at the American Embassy in Ivory Coast insisted he would not let the boys travel because of an immigration technicality, Mary Ann contacted Congressman Sidney Yates of Illinois and got the statesman to push past the bureaucratic red tape. Yates made a series of contacts that ultimately led to Secretary of State James Baker who, in turn, sent a telegram to the U.S. Consulate in Ivory Coast who, finally, at long last, granted the boys permission to travel. It was Sidney Yates, though, who heard Mary Ann's plea and pushed through the apathy and the international logjam.

"We are so grateful to you," Mary Ann wrote Congressman Yates upon the boys' arrival in the United States. "It's truly unusual to find caring, sensitive people who actually want to help Liberians." Yates was himself the son of immigrants, the youngest of six children born of parents from Lithuania. He grew up in Chicago and graduated from the prestigious University of Chicago and later earned a law degree. At the age of forty, he was elected to the U.S. House of Representatives and ultimately became the tenth longest-serving member in the history of the U.S. Congress. Later in his career, he was awarded the Presidential Citizens Medal by Bill Clinton and a government building in Washington, D.C. was named after him. In many ways, he embodied the American ideal of someone from an immigrant family who worked hard and made himself successful. There's little doubt his own life experiences made him sympathetic to the plight facing Rosetta and her boys. He was the right person at the right time with the right story. After getting one door after another slammed in her face, Mary Ann found the man who cared enough to do the right thing and allow a desperate mother to bring her boys to the safety of the United States.

The connectedness of all these stories is hard to overlook. It also makes the story feel even more perilous. If Mary Ann Taylor had not been at a church with a man who was born in Liberian and made them aware of the plight of the Liberian refugees, would Rosetta have had the advocate she needed? If Mary Ann had not gotten the attention and empathy of Congressman Sidney Yates, himself the son of immigrants, would there have been enough political muscle to get the job done? These are impossible questions to answer, but it is clear that the exact right people had to be at the exact right place and time for it all to work out. However, that is exactly what happened.

Mary Ann operated behind the scenes, but she was a major player in the human drama of the story of Yu-jay, Jared, and Rosetta and their struggle to get to a new land of safety and opportunity. Because of her tenacity, the visas were issued and the boys were free to travel to the U.S. to start a new life.

Later, Yu-jay said of both Mary Ann and Tom, "The Taylors inspired my passion for helping people of all races, creeds, and so on. We never felt anything but love—genuine love—when we were around them. They took us into their home, fed us, spent money on us, invested in us, and helped us get our footing."

Thanks in part to Mary Ann's doggedness, the boys were now coming to America, leaving behind the terror of the civil war. They had no idea what new challenges awaited them.

---

[1] Tubman died in office on July 23, 1971.
[2] Mary Ann had no way of knowing that Air Afrique was in serious debt at the time, losing millions of dollars per year. It eventually went out of business in 2002.

13

COMING TO AMERICA

"Part of America's genius has always been its ability to absorb newcomers, to forge a national identity out of the disparate lot that arrived on our shores."
- President Barack Obama

The transcontinental jet that brought Yu-jay and Jared to the U.S. had turbines that were taller than one grown man standing on another man's shoulders. The cabin was sprawling and spacious with three wide sections for passenger seating. The enormous airliner was intimidating to these boys who had never been in a plane before, but it felt sturdy and safe. It also represented hope. Once aloft, the plane would bring them to a new place brimming with opportunity and promise. For Yu-jay, coming to America was a dream come true.

"It meant coming to America, this sort of nirvana, the ultimate destination," he said. "It meant a new start. It meant putting all of the stuff behind you. It meant feeling safe again and not looking over your shoulders. It meant not worrying about if somebody is trying to take your life or if your life is in danger."

In other words, it meant everything to him and his family.

They landed at JFK airport in New York in the middle of April 1991. The moment they stepped off the plane was the coldest either of them had ever been in their lives. Yu-jay remembers both of them shivering and the people who were gathered to greet them wrapping them up with more and more layers.

"I think people were just throwing coats around us and we were doubling and tripling our shirts," he recalled. "We had never experienced such cold weather before." Reflecting on the day, Yu-jay compares it to a scene from the movie Cool Runnings, loosely based on the true story of the Jamaican men's national bobsled team first competition in the 1988 Winter Olympic Games in Calgary, Alberta, Canada.

Learn More

Family and friends took them into their home, where the boys stayed indoors nearly the whole time, huddled near the heater and sticking close to their mom. It was also the first time Yu-jay and Jared had ever seen snow.

"That was pretty wild. It was very different," he said of the snow. "I remember thinking it was very cold for two boys just coming from Africa," he said.

Yu-jay recalled the first thing he did upon arriving in New York City.

"We went to KFC and I think we each got a bucket," he said, adding, "It was great chicken."

After spending two weeks in the New Jersey area, the boys loaded on a Greyhound bus bound for Charlotte. They arrived on April 26, 1991 on Yu-jay's fifteenth birthday. Two years earlier, he had celebrated his birthday at his beautiful home in Liberia, surrounded by friends and family, unaware that the war would soon engulf all of them and change their lives forever. Two years earlier, he never would have imagined he would be arriving in a large city in the southeastern United States, about to restart his life.

Yu-jay also recalled it being bitterly cold when they arrived—or at least that is how he perceived it. In reality, the temperature averaged 62 degrees that day and never got below 50 degrees. Even though it was a far cry from the cold and snow of New Jersey they had just experienced, it was something they still had not gotten fully adjusted to, not in the two weeks they had stayed in Trenton, New Jersey. For all of them, their first days and weeks in the United States were remembered as much for the teeth-chattering cold as for the overload of new experiences.

Being in the United States was incredibly wondrous

and strange for them—and a complete shock to the system. For Yu-jay, it was like what he saw on TV, what he imagined the U.S. to be like. They were in a big city with tall buildings and shopping malls and huge supermarkets. Even the humans looked different, not just because most of them were white, but, as he put it, "people looked more healthy—and shiny!"

Yu-jay wondered if his mom had pictured this as a land of opportunity at the time, or just a place where they could all be together.

"I'm almost pretty certain there was a little bit of, 'You're in America and anything can happen.'"

Here they were in this new world of opportunity and adventure. They had no idea what was ahead of them. They couldn't even dream of what their lives would be like in the years to come.

They stayed with the Taylors for a few weeks when they first arrived in Charlotte. Mary Ann, of course, baked them a cake when they arrived. Now living in her home, the Liberian family got to experience Mary Ann's hospitality in person.

"She made me and Jared feel comfortable and loved," Yu-jay said, then added, "She made the best bran muffins! I used to enjoy just having them with orange juice when we first got there." This experience of American family life set a good template for Yu-jay and helped shape his own family customs later in life.

After the Taylors, they lived with a series of other individuals and families for a while. After bouncing around from place to place, they eventually got their own apartment in a tough neighborhood along Central Avenue in Charlotte. Central Avenue in Charlotte is a melting pot of a boulevard with Nepali refugees in one apartment complex, Vietnamese people in others, Hispanic folks, African-Americans, and other Africans. The place was home to many poor families, including Yu-jay and Jared and Rosetta.

"We had very little," Yu-jay recalled. "Simple life, you know, the three of us together."

His mother bought their first car for a few hundred dollars while they were there. It was a rickety old car that backfired randomly like an old jalopy, but it seemed to fit the run-down neighborhood that they now called home. While there were other neighborly Liberians who lived downstairs in the same building, it was still a rough area. In some ways, it was almost as scary as what they had escaped in Liberia.

"I couldn't imagine living there now with my family," he said. "It's a tough neighborhood. You would hear gunshots and stuff like that at night."

They had gone from being a well-off family in a poor country to a poor family in an affluent country. Now they had to rely on the goodwill of others to furnish their apartment or rummage around to find discarded items. Yu-jay found an old headboard for a bed that someone had thrown out and he brought it back to the apartment. Doing something like that would have been unthinkable in their lovely home in Monrovia, but here in this poor, rundown part of town, it was a necessity.

Yu-jay and Jared both enrolled in Eastway Middle School, a public middle school with a reputation for being

Learn More

rough and rowdy. Yu-jay immediately felt out of place with his thick Liberian accent and his lack of socialization to American culture. He talked fast and unintentionally used phrases the American kids didn't understand.

Jared, by contrast, couldn't wait to be an American and took to the culture and the dialect quickly. His acculturation to the school and the culture was rapid. His accent smoothed out quickly; his behavior and speech became more quickly Americanized.

Jared adapted to the tough environment, but Yu-jay struggled to fit in. The African-American students at Eastway were especially hard on him.

"Hey, Kunta! Kunta Kinte!" one kid yelled at him, referring to the real-life African character from the television mini-series Roots.

"Hey, man, you got a tail?" another one asked him, implying he was a monkey from Africa.

Eastway was a tough place for any kid. At the time, even the faculty weren't always safe. During a hallway altercation, a student punched a teacher square in the mouth and the man began to bleed. Yu-jay was dumbfounded by the assault. A child would never dare talk back to an elder in his culture. To assault a person in authority would be unthinkable.

Learn More

"There was very much a respect for your elders and their life experiences in Liberia," he said. No child would dare to even speak rudely to an adult in his country, but here in the United States, children cussed principals, defied parents, even hit teachers. It was appalling and inconceivable.

Worse yet, he even knew of other kids who had brought guns to school. There were fights and drug-dealings and arrests. One student committed suicide outside of the school during that year. The specter of violence always seemed to be roiling just under the surface.

"Just things like that, that I had never seen," he said. "This is America, you know? The land of milk and honey. These kids, what problems do they have? It was really weird and disturbing."

Even as a middle schooler, Yu-jay was aware of the opportunities that anyone could have in America and the help that people could get when they were at a disadvantage, so he found it to be terrifically confusing to see his peers who had chances at success, yet weren't making the most of them.

"In America, when you're poor, there is still hope. In Africa when you're poor, it's hopeless," Yu-jay said, recalling the words of Oprah Winfrey after a trip she took to South Africa to start a school for girls. "With these kids, what's going on over here? Punching your teacher? Fighting your principal? People getting killed. Gangs. There were so many kids who just looked so lost."

With the challenges of having so many disruptive and unruly kids around him, Yu-jay kept his head down and excelled in school at Eastway. He made the Honor Society and collected many of the other academic awards and honors they had there.

Despite being a tremendously social and outgoing person, Yu-jay didn't make good friends at Eastway. It was the first time in his life when he didn't connect with his peers.

"I'd rather have no friends than bad friends," Yu-jay said later.

He focused on his academics and did his best in school, even when the kids around him didn't seem to care about school.

He did, however, make at least one good friend at church during this time. Not surprisingly, it involved a mutual connection to Liberia. That friend, Jamie Bowers, was not Liberian himself, but had strong connections to the country. Jamie's grandfather was the missionary who dispatched help when Pan Am Flight 151 crashed on the Liberian mountainside in 1951. His father was born and grew up in Liberia. Though he had never personally been to West African country, he felt a deep bond with it.

In the late 1980s, a few years before the war came to Monrovia, J Gbarbea, a high-ranking Liberian official, fled the country with his family following a failed coup attempt. His family attended a Sunday School class at First Baptist Church in Charlotte, the same class that had stirred Mary Ann Taylor to action when she helped Rosetta get the boys to the U.S. When Jamie heard Mr. Gbarbea's family was attending the same church, he was thrilled at the opportunity to meet a new family from Liberia.

He saw them and made his way over to the family

and introduced himself.

"My dad grew up in Liberia!" he told Tyrone, their son, on that first Sunday.

The following week, Tyrone and his family happened to be sitting directly behind the Bowers family during the church service. Jamie mentioned to his dad that the family was from Liberia. At the end of the service, Mr. Bowers turned around and greeted Mr. Gbarbea in Liberian English.

"Mr. Gbarbea almost fainted at the surprise!" Jamie said. "And after some conversation, we discovered the family connections. My parents were good friends of Tommy and Mary Ann Taylor. The Taylors had already intervened on behalf of the Gbarbea family to get them out of the country and into safety, much in the same way they had helped Rosetta and the boys during their time of need.

A few years later, Jamie met Yu-jay in the same church. Rosetta and the boys attended at the Taylors' invitation. More than two decades later, Jamie still remembers the first time he met Yu-jay and Jared.

"We met on a Sunday morning in the spring of 1991 in the old Fellowship Hall of First Baptist Church, when I was in the eighth grade" Jamie recalled. "I remember Rob Jones, the interim youth pastor bringing them through the door and straight over to me, probably because he didn't really know what to do with these African boys and figured that since my dad was born in Liberia, I'd know what to do."

Jamie didn't know what to do either, except to be friendly and welcoming and to help them navigate their new world. He quickly realized everything was new to Yu-jay and Jared: the worship style of the church they all attended, supermarkets, school, apartment living, and transportation. Nearly every aspect of life was a new experience.

"Yu-jay's accent was so thick I thought his name was 'Eugene' for the first few weeks," Jamie said. "I remember Yu-jay as being more quiet and more reserved and Jared as more outgoing. This changed as Yu-jay's true personality came out."

Jamie became close friends with both brothers. Just as the bond that Jamie Bowers' father shared with the Liberian village blacksmith was due in part to a great tragedy, Jamie himself also formed a strong bond with the Liberian brothers years later, due to events set in motion by the even greater tragedy of the Liberian civil war.

The brothers forged a friendship with Jamie in those early days in the U.S. They spent time hanging out, going to the movies and basketball games and youth group activities. That summer they went with the youth group to Atlanta for a Braves game and stayed in a hotel. Jamie accidentally bumped a glass in the middle of the night.

"I remember...Yu-jay and Jared both springing awake as their war instincts kicked in," he said.

Over the years, the friendship between Yu-jay and Jamie deepened. They spent countless hours talking about life and faith and politics and the future. Jamie saw Yu-jay's grace under pressure on several occasions, including once during a youth group retreat. The family they were assigned to stay with was clearly racist and didn't hesitate to express it.

"They were obviously uncomfortable with a black person in their house and made all of us—members of the youth group and the retreat leader—uncomfortable with their pointed questions and behavior," Jamie said.

What stood out to him, though, was how Yu-jay diffused the situation. He was quiet and polite and refused to respond to them in an angry and hostile way.

"He was undoubtedly hurt by the situation, but instead of lashing out, he chose to turn the other cheek and move on," Jamie added.[1]

---

[1] Jamie later found out that the family became "totally transformed" soon after that. He believes Yu-jay's graceful response to them played a big role in their change of heart.

14

AN UNEXPECTED OPPORTUNITY

"In the middle of difficulty lies opportunity."
- Albert Einstein

As Mary Ann became more aware of Yu-jay's ugly situation at Eastway, she began to orchestrate a way to get Yu-jay into a private school. Neither Yu-jay nor his mom had even considered it before the Mary Ann brought up the possibility. She and Tom saw him as a smart, motivated kid who deserved to be in an excellent school. They arranged for him to have an interview at Charlotte Country Day, a private school in town.

"The Taylors orchestrated the whole Country Day thing," he recalled. "They thought of it. I didn't wake up one day and say I wanted to go to Country Day and mom didn't either."

On the day of the interview, he was as sharply dressed as he could be at the time. He greeted the faculty with a smile, then told them his story and his dreams for his life. They were impressed. He did well in the interview, passed the entrance tests with flying colors, and had already performed well in an American public school, so he was granted admission.

"Here's a kid who has come to America a year or two ago from the war who seems to be seizing the opportunity, so that helped, too," he said of himself, imagining the internal process that led up to his acceptance at the prestigious school.

Charlotte Country Day is one of the most prestigious private schools in the country. It's typically referred to as one of the "Big Three" private prep schools in Charlotte, along with Charlotte Latin and Providence Day School. By any measure, it is an impressive school. Country Day was the first independent school in the Charlotte region and had the first International Baccalaureate Diploma program in the area. The school fields 72 sports teams each year for seventh to twelfth grade with 90% of its students participating in some kind of organized athletics. The Country Day campus is known for top-notch technology, fine arts, and athletic facilities. The school's faculty are an impressive bunch, as well, with a full quarter of them being published authors, nearly forty percent having received travel grants to 37 countries, and more than half of them holding graduate degrees.

The school's alumni roster boasts an Oscar-winner in Kristen Anderson-Lopez, the songwriter of Frozen's "Let it Go," as well as a multiple Grammy-nominee in Ed Cash. The alumni roster also boasts Molly Barker, founder of Girls on the Run, along with professional athletes, award-winning filmmakers, judges, and CEOs.

The school is impressive, but it comes at a price. Tuition is as high as or higher than many people pay for a college education, placing it well beyond the reach of most families, especially a poor family like Yu-jay's.

The following year, he started his new adventure at the private school. Instead of poor kids who were fighting their teachers, he was now around goal-oriented students from well-off families and who intended to go to top-ranked colleges and universities. At his public school, most of his peers came from fragmented families; many of the kids didn't know their fathers, while others had parents in prison or on probation. Now he went to school with a professional basketball team owner's children, the owner of a NASCAR team's child, as well as children of engineers and doctors and lawyers and CEOs. The contrast could not have been more stark.

What he observed in these kids was that nearly all of them seemed to have a sense of direction or "a beginning with an end in mind," as he would describe it. He realized he was lacking that trait and that he wanted it.

"I really looked at those guys and thought I want to

be like them," he said. "I didn't want to be like a professional athlete or whatever. I wanted to be like those guys. I came to appreciate the hard work."

Country Day was a refuge for him, but there were still little adjustments. Nearly all the students had much nicer clothes than he did. They had nicer gadgets. They wore braces. Yu-jay remembers "completely freaking out" at the sight of kids with braces.

"I thought they were like aliens," he said. "Like kids in America have metal teeth!"

That was just one of many little moments of culture shock, but he adjusted quickly and figured out how to navigate his new world. He learned to ask a lot of questions. He was always seeking information, trying to understand the new culture, wanting to get to know his new classmates and teachers. His English teacher and academic advisor, Mr. Chris Martin, called Yu-jay "the man of a thousand questions."

"I like to talk, so I ask a lot of questions," Yu-jay said in agreement. "I remember I asked Mr. Martin a lot of questions and I was always curious to learn about people and learn about their backgrounds and what they were about."

His curious and outgoing nature, along with his ability to be highly flexible, allowed Yu-jay to adapt quickly to these new, unfamiliar situations.

Not everyone at Country Day became his friend, though. Some were put off by the new kid who asked so many questions. Others didn't like him because they sensed a social rival in this friendly, upbeat new kid with the big smile and the easy laugh.

Sean was one of those kids. He was a popular African-American student at Country Day. He was well-liked and regarded as a superb athlete, playing on travel soccer teams with the wealthier kids. He had been at Country Day years before Yu-jay arrived. Socially, he was at the top of his game; he did well with girls and had many friends at the school. Then Yu-jay came along and unwittingly threatened his social role at Country Day. Yu-jay's gregarious and warm style meant he quickly became beloved at the school. He also joined the varsity soccer team, which further helped his social cred. He became a leader on campus, sang in the choir, made the honor roll, and befriended the girls. His popularity grew quickly. Unbeknownst to Yu-jay, this began to eat at Sean.

Yu-jay still sported his skinny, underfed, war-survivor frame and Sean was a much bigger kid, outweighing him by a good 30 pounds or more. Sean would use his superior size to bully and physically intimidate Yu-jay. One day in the fall during soccer season, Yu-jay walked past him in the hallway. Sean used his much bigger frame to slam Yu-jay into the lockers for no reason, then he walked away, looking back at a shocked and rattled Yu-jay with a menacing look on his face.

"I think Sean, probably without knowing it at the time, just felt threatened by me," he said.[2]

Despite the occasional bully like Sean, Yu-jay developed a solid core of good friends who were among the brightest and best-liked students at the school. Unlike at Eastway where he was called xenophobic names, the nicknames he got at Country Day were terms of affection.

"I remember this one girl, she used to call me the alphabet man because of my name, Yu-jay," he recalled with a laugh. That girl liked him, as did many of the other girls at his school. He found it easy to be friends with girls and dated a couple of them while in high school. One of his girlfriends, a young lady from another school, was so attractive some of the other guys were envious and wondered how he had landed a relationship with such a belle.

"I think there are girls who like the 'it' guys who are

---

[2] Yu-jay and Sean still see each other regularly in the community. Sean is married with a family and the two of them have a cordial relationship. "The past is in the past," Yu-jay said. "We were young. I have had to deal with other Seans in my life since coming to the U.S. I have had tensions at times in middle and high school, graduate school, and at work.

jocks or whatever," he said, "and I think there are girls who sort of like sweet guys who seem like they would be the nice gentlemen kind of guy. People always say good guys finish last, but I always say good guys finish first."

Instead of trying to impress girls or act aloof, he simply made a point of being genuine and true to himself.

"I always just sort of focus on being me and that made me a lot of friends. Girls liked that. I didn't have any problems."

The time at Country Day was rich in relationships of all kinds. He had girlfriends, mentors, coaches, and close friends. He became connected with all kinds of people, including a self-described "redneck" and others who were much different than he was in nearly every way. He'd show genuine interest in people. He wanted to know them, to understand them, to connect with them.

"That sort of thing happened to me a lot in high school. You talk to people and make these weird connections and that ends up blossoming into a beautiful friendship," he said.

Some of the friendships he made at Country Day have served him for a lifetime. They had fun together, but they also challenged each other.

"I developed a pretty nice core group of friends who

were some of the nicest and brightest kids in school and just liked me for me," he said.

One of those extraordinarily bright kids was Carsten Weber. Yu-jay first met him in tenth grade at Charlotte Country Day School after Carsten had just switched schools and was still getting acclimated to his new surroundings. Yu-jay was also relatively new to the school, so they bonded over being the new kids. They also connected over being from different cultures. Carsten was born to a German family that had spent six years in Johannesburg, South Africa before coming to the United States.

"We both shared a curious but cautious view on the mainstream," Carsten said.

The two of them hung out many evenings, went on double dates, and enjoyed daily life at the school together. They were both active in the international students' club at school and helped organize several events. The following year, they got involved in Model UN and represented Djibouti, a small country about the size of New Jersey on the Horn of Africa. The little sovereignty is nestled into the eastern side of Ethiopia and touched on opposite sides by Somalia and Eritrea. While Yu-jay is from West Africa and Djibouti is in East Africa, it seemed only fitting that he represent a tiny African country.

When they arrived for the conference, Carsten remembers being somewhat overwhelmed by the spectacle in front of him. He sat back and listened to the different delegations discussing their plans and drafting resolutions.

"I was quite intimidated by the whole atmosphere and knew early on that I would remain passive and not participate actively in the discussions," he said.

At first, Yu-jay acted the same way, holding back, observing without participating much. However, late in the process, close to the end of the discussions, Yu-jay raised his hand and made a short proclamation to the delegations. It was simply a brief statement that the two representatives from the small country of Djibouti were following the discussions with much interest and they wished for the other delegations to come to a successful resolution in the end. The statement had an unexpectedly strong impact.

"I remember people applauding afterwards, and in the closing session, Yu-jay even received an honorable mention for his short but boldly worded contribution," Carsten said, adding, "I believe that it is this willingness to be curious and open to new, unknown situations that has helped Yu-jay to become the person he is today and that I value so much."

The statement to the Model UN also illustrated Yu-jay's interpersonal style that has been so effective: hang back and observe, then make a decisive move when the time is right in a way that is other-centered, optimistic, and motivational.

Carsten underscored this, saying, "On the one hand, Yu-jay always kept a healthy and curious distance to his surroundings and formed his own way of thinking without being assimilated into the mainstream. I believe it was this combination (of traits) that gave the people around Yu-jay the sense that he was interested in them and also helped him go his own way and reach the goals he had set, first at college, then in his job, and, of course, in his family."

Despite the richness of his school life and his new friendships, Yu-jay still had to return to the apartment off of Central Avenue each night where the same crime and violence still surrounded him. The Taylors gave him a bike that he locked up outside, but it was soon stolen. The parking lot and the apartment complex often crackled with danger and violence.

"I remember hearing gunshots often and my family hitting the floor, reminiscent of our life during the war," he recalled.

He lay in his bed each night and tried to reconcile the two worlds he was living in at the time. One world was

Charlotte Country Day School where he was surrounded by wealthy, privileged, mostly white kids who seemed to have everything, at least in terms of material needs. The other world was his rundown apartment in a rough part of town. It was crowded, there were sounds of gunshots, and the sounds of constant bickering and screaming and fighting bled out of other people's apartments.

"They were broken people and families," he said, "yet some were good, hardworking people trying to make the best out of their lives. There were people like my mother who was trying to give her boys the best she could."

Yu-jay is a keen observer, though, and the more he pondered each night, the more he realized things were not always as they seemed in any arena. There were broken marriages, absent parents, low self-esteem, substance abuse, and other problems of the rich world, too. They might look different, but wherever there were humans, there were problems. The closer he got to the rich world or the poor world, the more he saw that people often had similar struggles at the root. We are all different, he surmised, but at our core, we are the same.

15

HIGHER EDUCATION

"Education is the most powerful weapon which you can use to change the world."
- Nelson Mandela

Even with the hidden challenges and the human struggles, Yu-jay realized Country Day represented an amazing gift and a priceless opportunity for him. He seized his chance with both hands. The longer he was at Country Day, the more he immersed himself in the school, soaking it all in. He not only participated in the model UN, but he played junior varsity and varsity soccer, sang in the lead choir, served as vice-president of the International Student Association, and was active in and out of the classroom. By the time graduation came, he had won several awards at the school, including a top leadership award, and had solid grades, making him highly competitive for some of the best colleges in the country. At Country Day, it's expected that nearly all of the graduates go on to college, including Ivy League and other top-tier schools. But when the time came, neither Yu-jay nor Rosetta knew much about the process of getting into college, nor did they have the money for him to go to any school much beyond a community college or a technical school.

"You're probably going to have to go to community college or something," Rosetta said to Yu-jay.

Yet his counselor at Country Day, Ms. Anne Murphy, kept prodding him to dream of something bigger.

"Yu-jay, you can get into any school you want. Any school!" she said emphatically.

With his mom suggesting he may have to settle for community college, and his school counselor telling him he should shoot for the moon, he had no idea what to do. Was Ms. Murphy just being nice and encouraging or was she speaking the truth?

In addition to these voices in his head, Yu-jay also had two outside influences who swayed him to apply to their schools. Tom Taylor, one of his early champions, went to North Carolina State as an undergraduate and played baseball there. He later went to Duke for his master's degree and then earned a PhD from Pittsburgh. Of those schools, he had an emotional connection to Duke, so he would take Yu-jay there to visit, including once when they watched a home football game on campus.

Around the same time, the father of a Country Day friend named Ian, who was the CEO of a large data storage company called Verbatim America LLC, took the boys to help out at Davidson during the NCAA Men's national soccer championship tournament. Verbatim was a big sponsor of Davidson's soccer team and was also a major sponsor of the men's NCAA tournament, so Ian and Yu-jay got to experience some spectacular sporting events at the college for two years in row. Yu-jay first came to know the school and the campus, not so much through its superior academics, but through its soccer program. It was apparent, though, that Ian's dad thought he belonged there.

With all the competing opinions swirling in Yu-jay's head, his high school advisor and English teacher, Chris Martin, eventually stepped in and became the quarterback of Yu-jay's college application process, guiding Yu-jay through the process, weighing the options, sifting through the possibilities.

Chris taught English at Charlotte Country Day School and had taken a quick liking to Yu-jay and became committed, along with a handful of other teachers and administrators, to getting this amazing kid into a top-notch college. He imagined Davidson, one of the best small liberal arts colleges in the country, would be a great fit for him.

On one beautiful autumn day, Chris drove Yu-jay to Davidson to visit the school and interview with the admissions staff. Though it was less than an hour from his apartment, the beautiful campus and the quaint town seemed like another world away. The town of Davidson is a little hamlet of around 10,000 citizens that sits beside Lake Norman. Its motto is "College Town. Lake Town. Your Town." With tree-lined streets, classic architecture, and cozy shops, it is indisputably one of the most beautiful little towns in the southern U.S.

Before the college visit, they dropped in to see a friend of Chris' who lived there in town. Yu-jay sat on the front porch absorbing the sights and sounds of this quiet little southern town: birds chirping, squirrels scampering across the lawn and racing up trees, gentle winds, the fall of autumn leaves. Behind them in the distance, a train whistled as it rumbled through the town. After it passed, the whole place was quiet again. The whole world seemed completely still, hushed and soundless, at peace.

Yu-jay turned to Chris and said, "This is the most peaceful place I've ever been." It was the quietest moment he had ever had.

"I knew right away that he would be there at Davidson a year later," Chris said. He could tell Yu-jay had his heart on Davidson. He was also sure the brilliant, affable kid would be admitted to the prestigious school.

"I had the utmost confidence," he said. "I knew all

along his story was so great. He wasn't going to have any trouble."

As Chris sensed, it was love at first sight. Yu-jay fell in love with Davidson, the college and the town. When the time came early in his senior year, he applied for early admission to Davidson and got accepted, just as Mr. Martin had predicted. But not only was he admitted, he essentially got a full ride with enough scholarships and financial aid to leave him with only about $7,000 in student loans to repay for attending this outstanding school that easily costs over $40,000 per year. The college decision was clear.

Yu-jay took a psychology class his freshman year at Davidson. Almost immediately he realized it was a good fit for him. He had always been fascinated with behavior and the ways that people thought and acted. He frequently asked himself—and others—why people were the way they were. For him, it began with asking why he was the way he was, then it allowed him to ask why others had turned out as they had. Moving into a new country and trying to fit into a new culture made him curious to understand how people think, what made them different, and what connected them to each other. The class scratched that itch with its discussions of group dynamics and human behavior. He decided to major in psychology.

"It just seemed to be a really good fit for me and I decided to do it," he said.

He developed strong friendships in college, but he didn't tend to be drawn toward large groups and parties. Instead, he found himself being drawn much more to hanging out with one or two friends at a time and having deep, meaningful conversations. In return, this helped him get to know himself even better.

"In college, I think you start to learn about yourself," he said.

Part of that self-awareness was also some insight into his own personal limitations. Even more so than when he was at Country Day, he was around others who were his peers intellectually. They were highly motivated, extraordinarily capable people, among the brightest students in the country. Being surrounded by these outstanding individuals made him reflect on himself.

"I think God created each of us with limits, capabilities and unique talents," he said. "I don't think I could wake up tomorrow and say I want to be a neurophysicist or a rocket scientist. It would probably just be like trying to push a boulder up a hill."

But instead of being discouraged by this insight, it actually liberated him. It gave him more clarity in understanding his own strengths and talents, while allowing him to acknowledge his own limitations. He didn't have to be the best at everything, to excel at everything, he quickly realized. He just needed to know himself and his own personal gifts and passions.

Davidson was academically rigorous and stressful at times, but it was also one of the most relaxed times in Yu-jay's life. The peaceful village proved to be a respite for him.

But even at Davidson, which was a known for being an open-minded liberal arts college, one white hall mate called him a "token black" who was only admitted to help the school meet its quota. The other kid went on to say that Yu-jay hadn't earned admission to the school like he had, despite the fact that he knew nothing of Yu-jay's academic credentials or track record. On another occasion, a Hispanic student called him the n-word. In both instances, other African-American students who were nearby came to his defense.

Learn More

"These experiences marked my beginning of understanding the racially-charged world I live in," he said.

He understood poor, unruly kids at Eastway Middle making prejudiced and derogatory comments, but he had a much harder time comprehending how college-educated people could say those things. If these kinds of comments were being made at liberally-minded Davidson, imagine what other people were saying—and thinking—about him beyond the campus.

Still, he persisted in making friends with people of all races and backgrounds. He became close friends with a South Korean guy named Kenny Lee. The two of them were roommates at Davidson and shared a love for piping hot kimchi noodles.

"It was almost like he cooled the noodles as he ate ," Yu-jay said. "It was amazing, he had obviously eaten this his whole life. I would be on my second bite and he would be done. That stuff was hot!"

Yu-jay immersed himself in understanding different cultures and building relationships with people from all kinds of backgrounds. As a refugee from a war-torn, third world country coming to an affluent nation, he had a unique perspective that allowed him to understand and connect with a wide range of people. He took a position as a pre-orientation counselor at Davidson that further exposed him to students from different backgrounds. It was through that job that he met a young lady who would play a key role in his adult life. Her name was Nena.

16

A GIRL NAMED NENA

"Happy is the man who finds a true friend, and far happier is he who finds that true friend in his wife."
- Franz Schubert

Nena grew up on the eastside of Charlotte with her mother and three brothers. Her father lived at home with them during her early years, but by the time she was seven years old, he had moved out. Soon after that, he moved to New York city, only seeing his kids on rare occasion. One summer when Nena was around 12 years old, she and her two younger brothers visited her father in New York. It was the last time she ever spent extended time with him.

Nena's mother was left to raise four children—Nena, her older brother, and two younger ones—on her own and life was hard for Nena and her siblings growing up in a single-parent home. Money was tight and the neighborhood was unsafe. Many times, her mother would work two jobs just to keep food on the table.

Her father rarely sent money unless he was forced to do so by the court and even then, there were times when he did not work, so he had no income to help provide for the children. Nena's paternal grandmother and her maternal grandfather helped the family survive. They would help the kids buy clothes when they needed them. The struggling family also received help from other extended family members along the way, including other aunts and uncles. Her grandfather would pick the kids up from daycare when her mother could not. Nena remembers visits from her grandfather as the highlight of the week.

"We could hear his truck coming down the road and we would run outside to meet him in the yard," she said.

Her mother was a proud woman who didn't ask for help unless she was desperate. She rarely complained about her struggles or asked others for support.

"She was stoic," Nena said, "and she did what she needed to do to keep food on the table and a roof over our heads."

Nena learned a sense of responsibility from her mother, but she also was thrust into adult-level responsibilities at a young age. As early as 11 years old, she would babysit her cousins during the summer months when all the kids were out of school, sometimes watching upwards of ten children at a time, along with her two younger brothers.

"That taught me great responsibility, to be in charge of that many kids all day," she said. "I enjoyed school and looked forward to learning. I was always a star student and my teachers showered praises on me. I tried very hard to do well and remember shedding tears if I did not believe my work was good enough."

Nena credits her mother, the woman who raised four children and worked tirelessly to provide for them without complaining, with giving her a sense of independence and grit. Her mother was, in all ways, a great role model for her daughter.

"Even as a young girl, I did not give up on difficult things easily," she said, adding that she was by nature introverted, which seemed to make her less vulnerable to negative peer influence. She didn't seek the approval of her classmates or other kids in her neighborhood. She was content to focus on schoolwork and creating a good future for herself.

Nena also had several teachers along the way who instilled confidence in her and encouraged her to become a leader. Her high school health occupations teacher nurtured her interest in the healthcare field, in particular. Her student council advisor pulled her out of class one day and asked her to run for student body president.

"I never would have volunteered for that position," she said, "but she saw something in me that I did not see in myself. Until that point, I did not think of myself as a leader, but I became one because of her."

She did, in fact, become the student body president of Garinger High School, thanks to the urging of her teacher. She was also the captain of her school's varsity cheerleading team, played on the girls' varsity soccer team, and was an officer in another club that same year.

After high school, Nena faced many challenges, including family deaths and financial hardships. She had to work full-time to be able to support herself during those years. In addition to the great example and model set by her mom, she credits her relationship with God as a source of strength.

"I knew that God had a great plan for me. There were times when I felt like giving up, but I knew I had to keep fighting," she said.

This faith sustained her through college and when she faced other hardships and obstacles. Her faith, her mother, and the support of peers and colleagues helped her keep going when she didn't think she had it in her.

She took a rather circuitous route to Davidson, the school where she and Yu-jay would meet. During her senior year of high school, she received the Pearl S. Buck Award from Randolph College, formerly Randolph-Macon Woman's College. She was invited to visit the school and was immediately smitten with the college. It had a beautiful campus, a small student-to-faculty ratio, and the feeling of belonging to a sisterhood. Having grown up with no sisters, the idea of going to an all-women's college was extremely appealing to her. She attended the school and loved it, but her scholarship was only for one year and when it ran out, she didn't have the funds to return the following year.

"I made the hard decision to take a year off in order to work and save money with plans of returning," she recalled. "I was trained as a certified nurse assistant during that time and worked hard to save up money."

However, as the time drew closer for her to return, she still did not have enough money to cover the cost of attending. A former high school teacher encouraged her to apply to Davidson College instead because Davidson was known for offering strong financial aid packages, in addition to its reputation for academic excellence. She applied and was accepted. Not only that, but she was given a generous financial aid package. She remembers being in tears and being thankful to God when she heard the news.

"My year off had been filled with doubt and uncertainty," she said. "At one point I had decided I did not need to go back to college. I was the first one in my family to go to college and that value was not something that was instilled in me. I was working and making money."

Despite this, she remembers the day she realized she needed to go back. She overheard another nurses' assistant discussing her hourly wages. The nurse had been there almost 20 years and was only making about 50 cents more per hour than Nena was.

"I knew right away that, as thankful as I was to have worked in that role, this could not be the only thing that I was called to do," she recalled. "So I accepted admission to Davidson College as a transfer student and started my sophomore year there in the fall of 1997."

Had she not made the decision to attend Davidson, it is highly unlikely she would have ever met Yu-jay. The two first met at the college's pre-orientation. It was an event held specifically for African-American students who were just started their college careers there.

"I was there with the entering freshmen," she said. "Yu-jay, along with some other upper classmen, was serving as a counselor and mentor. He was in one of the small groups for one of the activities that we had."

Not surprisingly, he was extremely nice and seemed genuinely interested in what each person in the group had to share and contribute to the group. But despite that favorable first impression, there was no spark between them.

"In the close-knit community that was typical of Davidson, we were never anything more than brief acquaintances," she said.

In the spring of Yu-jay's senior year, Nena became the Resident Advisor for her dorm. She had coordinated a hall program with Yu-jay's dorm. The two of them began talking a little during that event.

"We laughed easily together and our backgrounds were similar," she said.

Then tragedy struck: Nena's father had slid into a deep depression, and ended up taking his own life.

In one moment of horror, Nena lost her estranged father she was starting to reconnect with after he moved back to Charlotte from New York.

Yu-jay learned about the event from a professor. The teacher shared that this girl, Nena, had experienced a sorrowful loss and would be out of school for a while.

"I remember I started sharing with her some of the stuff I went through, and just really trying to be a friend," he recalled.

Their relationship evolved from there. "It wasn't one of those things that was love at first sight because I wasn't looking for love," he said. "I just felt like, wow, she has been through so much. I just lent a hand, listened, tried to be a friend, and it went from there."

Nena and Yu-jay bonded over their similar backgrounds. They both were raised by single mothers and they both experienced tragic events. For Yu-jay, it was surviving the Liberian civil war; for Nena, it was the suicide of her father. These events gave both of them a sense that life is short, that every day is a gift, and that you have to make each day count.

Spending more time together, they realized they had stronger feelings for each other that extended beyond friendship.

"I was at a place in my life where I was intentionally trying to avoid any dating relationships, so I was hesitant to be more than friends," she said.

The relationship naturally grew deeper and feelings grew stronger. They seemed made for each other. They laughed a lot together. They shared common interests and a deep faith.

Yu-jay knew she was the one. He proposed to Nena on July 3, 1999 at her grandfather's birthday celebration and she accepted. Their marriage happened quickly by most standards. Even though they both grew up with single moms and felt ill-prepared for marriage, they shared a faith that sustained and gave them a sense of hope and mutual purpose.

Despite having these deep bonds and common connections, they knew marriage would be a challenge. They were extremely different personalities. Yu-jay was extremely extroverted; Nena was quiet and reserved. Yu-jay had a more indirect style of confrontation, whereas Nena was much more direct and confrontational. Yu-jay liked to talk; Nena liked to be quiet and think.

"If I could just find a way to shut up, I think our marriage would be a lot better," he said with a smile.

The two of them make a good contrasting pair. She tends to hide her accomplishments, rarely letting others know of her impressive accomplishments; Yu-jay tends to brag. She is cautious and deliberate; he is more of a risk-taker who is apt to throw caution to the wind. She is more introverted and quiet; he is extroverted and has never met a stranger.

"We are learning to value one another's perspectives," she said. "I like to think I have helped him to mellow out over the years!"

Despite this mellowing, she believes he still feels pressure to make each day better than the one before. She finds herself nudging him not to get bogged down in "quality improvement," but she knows that he carries a tremendous burden for people—especially his Liberian family, including his extended family—and people he finds in palpable need. She says he "often feels guilty that he cannot help everyone. There are so many that depend on him for support and just that realization challenges his sense of 'doing the best by his people.'"

Both of them share an unfailing work ethic and a deep commitment to those they love. They have obvious differences of personality and style, but they are bonded by the deeper things.

"You know, we share the most critical things—out faith, our values, our family, shared dreams," he said. "To me, if you can agree on the big things, you can work through the little things."

17

MORE BLUE-SKY TRAGEDY

"Although the world is full of suffering, it is full also of the overcoming of it."
- Helen Keller

"What I remember about 9/11 was how beautiful that day was," said a woman who witnessed the attacks on the World Trade Center. "It was a perfect morning. The sky was that deep blue you only see in September. There wasn't a cloud in the sky. And then..."

It sounds like an almost identical description of how Yu-jay and Jared described the morning the soldiers exploded through their front door. A seemingly calm, beautiful day shattered by an unthinkable act of terror. While everyone in the U.S. was shaken by the 9/11 trauma, one can only imagine what it does to someone who had already lived through the violent and unexpected start of a war.

Two years earlier, Yu-jay had graduated college. Davidson proved to be as good an experience as he had hoped. He met lifelong friends, found his wife, was active in the campus community, and hauled in great grades. He left as a Bonner Scholar, one of only a handful of students to have a four-year scholarship based on leadership ability and the desire to make positive community change. He was also listed in Who's Who of American College Students and had only amassed less than seven thousand dollars in college loans.

During his senior year, he interned for a Fortune 100 company and they promptly offered him a job upon graduation. Stepping out as a recent graduate, he was more than set. He had already secured an outstanding job and wasn't weighed down with any serious debt. He was ready to tackle the work world.

In the fall of 2001, he was doing well and making good money. He and Nena had found their rhythm as a married couple. Life was good and predictable and safe, at least until that horrible Tuesday morning.

He was in his office early, already dug into his work for the day. A colleague named Karen worked in the office beside his and she always kept her radio on through the workday.

Without warning, she frantically yelled for him and called him into her office.

"Yu-jay! Yu-jay, did you hear the news?" she began. "A plane just crashed into the World Trade Center."

They hurried to the conference room and turned on the television just in time to see the second plane slamming into the South Tower. Soon afterwards, a plane went down in a field in Pennsylvania, though the reports at the time were unclear and contradictory. Another plane hit the Pentagon. There was immediate panic and confusion. There were reports (later confirmed false) that a car bomb had gone off at the U.S. State Department Headquarters and that another Delta Airlines flight had been hijacked. Information and misinformation was coming in fast and furious. The whole world watched as the South Tower of World Trade Center collapsed a minute before 10:00 a.m. Less than a half hour later, the North Tower collapsed. It was nothing short of a nightmare.

Yu-jay felt electrified with horror. His boss sent everyone home and they all quickly dispersed to be with their loved ones. Walking out, Yu-jay was numb and in shock, as if he was living a bad dream. He got into his car and immediately began to cry. He sobbed all the way home.

It isn't hard to understand why the events of September 11 hit anyone hard. It was the biggest act of terror in all of modern times. But Yu-jay wondered why it was shaking him so intensely, striking him at the very core of his being. Then it became more clear to him.

"Because it felt like all those things were going away," he said, referring to the terrors of war and violence. "Now it was like full circle. I didn't feel safe anymore. I'm a grown man now and 9/11 shook me at my core."

He felt like he had left the violence and the never-ending sense of feeling unsafe behind him. Over the years, he had adjusted to the relative safety and calm of life in the United States. He could sleep soundly at night without gunfire down the street or in the parking lot. He was able to pursue his dreams and passions without fear that it would be ripped away from him as it had been before from his mother and his family.

"Then I see all this happen and I felt completely insecure again," he said. "And I just remember crying. I will never forget that."

More years passed and the country had immersed itself in two wars in response to the terrorist attacks. The economy had been shaky and the national climate was tense and contentious, but the sense of safety slowly began to return to the nation and to Yu-jay personally. The traumatic experience let him know that while he had left the war, the war had not fully left him.

After a few years of work, he began thinking about next steps for him. At both Country Day and Davidson, he had been in academic environments where the students had lots of big thoughts. Many of his friends were finishing college the same time he was and were moving on to pursue graduate school, working toward master's degrees and PhDs. He wasn't sure that he really wanted a master's degree or not, but he knew he wanted to be competitive. He wanted to keep up with his friends—and his super-high-achieving wife, for that matter! More importantly, he wanted more responsibility in his work. He wanted to understand the big picture in the world of business, so he applied to the competitive MBA program at UNC-Chapel Hill. He was accepted and made his plans to start the program in the fall of 2004.

Attending his first class on the fabled Chapel Hill campus, he was struck by the importance of this new milestone. Now here was a young man who was born to a poor, single, teenage mom in a third world country, he thought. He had lived in abject poverty in his early years. He had experienced a brutal war where he had seen people killed. He had become a refugee and had made his way to the United States, worked hard in school, had graduated from one of the best liberal arts colleges in the country, and was now enrolling in one of the top twenty MBA programs in the world.

"I always measured myself against kids who had significantly more than I had," he said, "but I think in doing that, I sort of raised the bar for myself and I think there is power there."

He chose business school because he liked corporate

America and enjoyed learning about business. He liked understanding how businesses work and what could make them better. He especially liked the marketing side of business because it also relied on his psychology background. It made him think about how businesses big and small could get consumers to want their goods and services.

By this time, his life experiences had allowed him to be so acutely tuned in to the human experience that this was now second nature to him. He understood how other people thought. He could see what motivated them. And he could do this with a range of people from different ethnic and cultural backgrounds. His innate flexibility had allowed him to become so adept at reading others that it was a natural fit for marketing and other aspects of the business world.

"I've always been fascinated by people and what they want and who they are," he said. "That's why I decided to major in psychology. As I got older and got in college, I realized I liked business. I really had an interest in consumer psychology and what drives the consumer behavior. How you can create that stimulus that makes a product compelling and all that appeals to the rational and the emotional."

He saw business as a good and important part of the economic backbone of the country. He also believed businesses could be a force for good, providing people with products and services that make their lives better. Coming from a country without much, he didn't take for granted what he had—or could have—in the United States. The experiences of his youth made him more appreciative of the opportunities here and he saw the role of business through a positive lens.

He was proud of his accomplishments up to that point, but his experience in his MBA program was not entirely positive. The program drew highly ambitious, often intensely competitive students. Yu-jay had made an art form of disarming people and getting them to like him. For one of the first times in his adult life, he wasn't able to do that. He had been called names at Eastway and bullied by Sean, but those were just kids. Adults were much more reasonable—or so he thought.

"I don't like you," one classmate told him straight up.

"Uh, okay, but why?" he asked. He really wanted to know.

"You've got a chip on your shoulder," the guy said.

Yu-jay was stunned by the assertion. Having a chip on your shoulder meant you were holding a grudge, that you were bruising for a fight. He felt none of that.

"I really don't think I do," Yu-jay replied.

"You do," the guys said, dismissively. "You're full of yourself."

Though this wasn't the norm, he realized some cut-throat business people thrived on chopping others down to size. Whether it was the other guy's misperception or a tactic to rock him back on his heels, it rattled Yu-jay. It was so foreign to his own view of himself.

"Nobody ever told me anything like that before," Yu-jay said, recalling the interaction.

In this competitive academic environment, he was experiencing more interpersonal trouble than he had known before. Because of his open and gregarious nature, he wasn't used to people openly voicing dislike for him. It shocked him, but it also created a fresh insight for him.

"I realized that everybody doesn't like you and you can't please everybody, so you just have to do you," he said. For a person who banked on getting everyone to like him, this realization was profound. It would serve him well in the years to come in his career and in his relationships.

With a little wear and tear, he completed his MBA. Once again, he did well academically and was well-positioned for his next big step. He sorted through his options and took a job with Coca-Cola in Atlanta. The company was one of the crown jewels of the Empire City and the job was a plum position by any standard. Atlanta, with its towering buildings and tangled highways, was the largest city either he or Nena had ever lived in. There was so much to take in and explore. It felt like a great step in the adventure their life had become.

By this time, Yu-jay and Nena already had a son named Kyle and Nena was pregnant with their daughter. They had settled comfortably into their new routine and all seemed to be well until yet another terrifying moment struck out of the blue.

They had just enjoyed a little Super Bowl party with pizza and soda as they watched the Giants revel in their first Super Bowl victory. As with the other times when terror struck, the next morning seemed to be a beautiful, but unre-markable day. Yu-jay got up like any ordinary day and went to the gym as he did most days before work. He was doing circuit training, pushing himself hard without taking many breaks, sweating and straining.

Then without warning, he collapsed.

"I remember lying on the floor," he recalled, "and I wasn't completely out, but I couldn't move anything. I couldn't talk. I couldn't control anything. It was almost like total body paralysis. I remember thinking to myself, now I'm 30-something years old. I have a wife, I have a kid. . I remember thinking, 'Lord, I'm too young to die.' It was very scary."

He was rushed to the hospital. Early tests suggested that he might be having some serious heart problems and might even be in need surgery.

"He made need a pacemaker," one doctor told them.

It was a terrifying thought. From there, it was test after test. He was in the hospital for three full days as they ran one assessment after another. Finally, the verdict was in: he had just given out from overexertion and dehydration. His body was reeling from the collapse, but he was going to be okay.

That kind of experience has not happened to him before or since, but it was yet another time that caused him to re-evaluate his life and his priorities again. Yu-jay and Nena decided to return to Charlotte to be closer to their family and close friends.

He took a job back home working for the Lance Corporation in their marketing department. After a brief stint there, he eventually landed at Bank of America in consumer marketing where he continues to use his aptitude for both business and psychology in his daily work.

"I'm working a lot with strategies and ideas for getting people to deepen their relationship with us," he explained.

Deepening relationships is really what Yu-jay has

been about, whether with his family or close friends or any-one else in his sphere of influence. In later years, Yu-jay has developed a passion for mentoring. For him, it was a way of giving back and contributing to the lives of others in the same way that people had been so generous with him.

When he was in graduate school, he began attend-ing King's Park International Church, a multi-ethnic and multi-generational church in Durham, NC. Soon after he got there, he met a young man named Jordan Council. Jordan remembers when and where they met: it was in 2003 near the church bookstore. He recalls how at-ease Yu-jay seemed to be for a new member, seeming right at home at quick to offer help and friendship. As their friendship was forming, Yu-jay would frequent the local Starbucks where Jordan worked as a barista at the time. He said that Yu-jay had a gift for "making our stresses melt with his no-one-is-a-stranger ways."

Yu-jay learned that Jordan had grown up in the foster care system, having lived in a dozen or so foster homes. He saw in Jordan an incredible intelligence and a curious mind, calling him "a complex young man with a lot of depth." He began to invest himself in this talented guy with so much po-tential, much in the same way that others had done for him when he was younger.

Years later, Jordan had powerful words to say about Yu-jay.

"Few inspired me to learn new things more than Yu-jay. He showed me how broad knowledge and a gregarious disposition could build intimate relationships. With Yu-jay, you don't feel judged. Period. It doesn't matter who you are," Jordan wrote. Yu-jay, he said, "makes it all look easy. I may never know just how hard it was for him to get this far."

18

INVICTUS

Out of the night that covers me,
Black as the pit from pole to pole,
I thank whatever gods may be
For my unconquerable soul.

In the fell clutch of circumstance
I have not winced nor cried aloud.
Under the bludgeonings of chance
My head is bloody, but unbowed.

Beyond this place of wrath and tears
Looms but the Horror of the shade,
And yet the menace of the years
Finds, and shall find me, unafraid.

It matters not how strait the gate,
How charged with punishments the scroll,
I am the master of my fate:
I am the captain of my soul.
-William Ernest Henley

Why do some people experience the worst things in life—war violence, threat of death, constant terror—and come out relatively unscathed or even better than before, people like Yu-jay, while countless others develop post-traumatic stress disorder or other emotional and physical problems? Some are deeply affected for years, often decades, by the trauma they've experienced. It affects their sleep, their school and work performance, their self-esteem, their relationships, and their overall well-being. They are more prone to stomach problems and even neurological maladies. Severe and prolonged trauma can affect people in nearly every area of their lives. But there are others who not only survive those experiences, but actually become stronger and better versions of themselves.

Yu-jay was a sickly, asthmatic, self-described "mama's boy" who fled his house in dress shoes yet he traveled so far by foot he walked the heels off the shoes, showing more

Learn More

stamina than other, more fit people. He was held at gunpoint, minutes away from being murdered, yet he found his way out. He was bullied and intimidated, but he pushed even harder to do well in school. Even from a young age, there was something in him that was remarkably resourceful.

Some people possess traits that allow them to deal with the worst that life can offer and emerge on the other side as a stronger version of their former selves. Psychologists have been studying these types of people and their unique constellation of traits and have found answers to what separates those who do the best in the face of traumatic events and the others who don't fare as well.

For those more resilient individuals like Yu-jay, we

call this "post-traumatic growth." These are people who grow through hardship. They become stronger, more determined, more resilient, even more compassionate.

Ironically, the men who pioneered the field of post-traumatic growth, Dr. Richard Tedeschi and Dr. Lawrence Calhoun,1 live and work in the same town Yu-jay came to call his home. They are both professors at the University of North Carolina-Charlotte.

Dr. Tedeschi doesn't know Yu-jay, but when he learned of his story, he wrote,

"In this man's story it appears that a combination of active support from others (during the war, in the refugee camp, and in the US) was crucial in his survival and in his opportunity to thrive. I imagine he was grateful for these acts of kind support, that at some times put those who protected him in danger. He may have had a moral sense that...led him to foresee a greater purpose for himself. With gratitude built on a perspective developed from all of this, he becomes the man he is."

Dr. Tedeschi nailed the key elements of Yu-jay's resilience: support from others, gratitude, deep connection, and a sense of purpose. These all mixed together to shape a man who has seen the worst of humanity, yet embraces and embodies the best of humanity.

A powerful thread through Yu-jay's story is his strong connection and attachment to others, beginning with his mom, then extending to others, including teachers and mentors and friends. This theme of deep relational connection is found in nearly all stories of resilient people. One study of 482 children who had experienced war found that a third of them were classified as "resilient," those that had witnessed or experienced trauma but had emerged relatively unscathed.2 When they looked closer at what separated the resilient group from the traumatized group, they found that the quality of friendships was an important factor. These resilient kids had significantly better friendships than the other kids.

Another powerful theme that is found in Yu-jay's story is his seemingly undying optimism and positive outlook. You can imagine another person who had been threatened with death more than once, run out of their own home, lost everything, almost conscripted as a child soldier, spent time in a refugee camp, faced bullying and other indignities would have a cynical view of people and the world in general. Not so with Yu-jay. Despite the hardships, he remained positive and optimistic, believing in his ability to make his life better.

This optimism seems to be a common trait among those who do well in life, despite the hardships. A study found of people who had lived through war found that those who were more optimistic were also more likely to be spared much of the intense symptoms of anxiety and other mental distress that befell others who had gone through similar war trauma.3

There are also core personality traits that seem to predict how well someone will do in the face of hardship, trauma, and loss. Over the decades, psychologists have found that personality tests are all essentially measuring five human traits captured by the acronym OCEAN: openness, conscientiousness, extroversion, agreeableness, and neuroticism. Openness is a measure of intellectual curiosity, creativity, appreciation of new ideas, and enjoyment of art and aesthetics. Conscientiousness is a tendency to be organized and dependable, showing self-discipline. Extroversion is a measure of how socially outgoing a person is. Agreeableness is a person's tendency to be compassionate, trusting, and cooperative, rather than suspicious and antagonistic. Neuroticism is a measure of strong negative emotions and the ability to cope with those intense feelings.

One study of people who had experienced severe traumatic events concluded that individuals who were less conscientious and more neurotic tended to have worse mental health problems down the road. It would be expected, then, that Yu-jay would probably rate high in conscientious-ness and low in neuroticism. Without any knowledge of the research, Yu-jay completed a test measuring the OCEAN traits. His results lined up exactly as expected.

Yu-jay rated highly on Conscientiousness, meaning he is reliable and dependable. He sets clear goals and pursues them with grit and determination. It makes sense that peo-ple who are highly conscientious tend to do better in the face of severe hardship because they tend to have a greater sense of self-efficacy, a strong belief in one's own ability to reach goals. For these people, like Yu-jay, they are not just victims at the mercy of forces beyond their control. A person like this believes, in the words of William Ernest Henley's poem that began this chapter, "Invictus," "I am the master of my fate: I am the captain of my soul." Indeed, we know that it is exact-ly this mindset that helps many people not only survive, but thrive in the face of chaos and trauma.

It's not surprising that Yu-jay also scored low on Neuroticism, which means he tends to be exceptionally calm, cool, and unflappable. He doesn't tend to overreact to stress and he keeps his emotions even in situations that most peo-ple would be considered highly stressful.

In addition, Yu-jay's score on the Extroversion scale was very high, revealing what we already knew: he is outgoing, sociable, energetic, and lively. He draws energy from being around other people. That high sociability is likely what serves as some protection against the impact of intense trauma. People who have a high degree of social support and feel emotionally connected to others do better in the long-run when faced with extreme adversity. It follows that a highly extroverted person like Yu-jay would tend to have a greater degree of social support—and be willing to seek it out when it's needed.

That's what one of the leading researchers and thinkers on resilience, Dr. Robert Brooks, discovered in his study of the most resilient people. He found six mindsets that are characteristic of the most resilient people. Most of these ways of thinking—a view that good decisions lead to better life outcomes and a belief that mistakes are opportunities for growth and not just moments of shame—are exactly what we would expect of the people who overcome adversity and succeed in life. But there is one that is unexpected. What Dr. Brooks found was that the most resilient people are the most open to help and support.4

In the U.S., we have this notion that the strongest people are the most self-sufficient, the ones who pull themselves up by their bootstraps. Dr. Brooks and other psychologists have discovered that the most resilient are, in fact, the ones that let others help them and support them when they need it. They don't try to do it on their own.

Yu-jay was one of these people. He was a kid who let other people help him and support him. He accepted mentoring and input. He sought out wise advice.

"Yu-jay actively seeks out assistance, but also doesn't 'expect' help," said Jamie Bowers. He added, "Yu-jay cultivates a wide network of friends, mentors, and associates who can help him achieve spiritual, personal, family, and business goals. He isn't afraid to ask for advice or favors. However, he has never been a 'victim' dependent on others. He can use his unique background and struggles to identify needs and personal deficiencies, use his experience to secure a mentor or coach willing to help, but never expect to be carried as a birthright due to his difficult background."

Jamie went even further, sharing some profound insight into Yu-jay's character. Having been with him in many situations, sat with him in countless conversations, and observed him over the years, he knows him well. He explained the personal qualities that have help build and mold Yu-jay into the man he has become:

"Yu-jay looks forward and doesn't dwell on the past. Yes, Yu-jay reminisces about his life before the war. Yes, Yu-jay was hugely influenced by his experiences in the war, and as a refugee, and as a teenager suddenly transplanted to Charlotte. But he doesn't dwell on what was left behind, or missed out on, or the negative experiences he had. He accepts them, learns from them, and moves on."

Jamie goes on to list other factors that were significant in shaping Yu-jay: a great mother, a vibrant Christian faith, a strong advocate in Mary Ann Taylor, and a remarkable wife. Not surprisingly, all of these are different kinds of relationships, all of which played a vital role in his life.

This is Yu-jay's story, but it is also a tale of the others who walked beside him.

A peek into the lives of the most resilient people finds that nearly all of them, like Yu-jay, have significant people who surround them—friends, family members, mentors, coaches, clergy, educators. For Yu-jay, his life began with a close relationship with his mom, one that helped shape his personality and character. It continued forward with Jared and Sylvester and Moses and Mary Ann and Jamie and Carsten and Chris and Nena and many others. These people are all woven into the fabric of his very being.

Yes, this is Yu-jay's story, but it is also the tale of those who befriended him, challenged him, helped him, encouraged him, and loved him.

It's a story of how much we need each other.

---

[1]These two psychologists have written many articles and books on

the topic of Post-traumatic Growth, including their recent, Post-traumatic Growth in Clinical Practice.

[2] Resilience among children in war: The role of multilevel social factors. Peltonen, Kirsi; Qouta, Samir; Diab, Marwan; Punamäki, Raija-Leena Traumatology, Vol 20(4), Dec 2014, 232-240.

[3] Dispositional optimism and self–esteem as competing predictors of acute symptoms of generalized anxiety disorders and dissociative experiences among civilians exposed to war trauma. Weinberg, Michael; Besser, Avi; Zeigler-Hill, Virgil; Neria, Yuval Psychological Trauma: Theory, Research, Practice, and Policy, Vol 7(1), Jan 2015, 34-42.

[4] Dr. Robert Brooks has written extensively on resilience and the mindsets that foster resiliency. Check out The Power of Resilience: Achieving Balance, Confidence, and Personal Strength in Your Life.

19

THE CURTAIN CALL

"Be thankful that the road is long and challenging, because that is where
you'll find the best that life has to offer."
- Ralph S. Marston, Jr.

At the end of a good play, the actors come out and take their bows in what is called a "curtain call." Some of the best movies also end with a curtain call where all the major characters appear on screen once more. Think of Titanic where Rose and Jack meet again at the top of the staircase where he takes her hand and they embrace. We see all the major characters around them. Think of Lord of the Rings: Return of the King where Gandalf is surrounded by the Hobbits at the conclusion of the journey.

Yu-jay's story is so remarkable and epic that it's only fitting to give the main players their curtain calls.

Like some others in this story, Nena's story is so rich she deserves a biography of her own. When she was working on her first degree at Davidson, she traveled to Haiti during school breaks on service missions three separate times. She also went to Ghana for a 6-week summer service project. The following year, she went to Zambia for six weeks. During her time in Zambia, she was able to work with traditional birth attendants and nurses at the local hospital and in the outlying villages. It was there that she saw her first live birth and it solidified her decision to become a nurse-midwife.

When she was working on her first nursing degree, she became a volunteer doula, someone who assists women in labor. During her midwifery program, she earned two academic and leadership awards named after legendary midwives: The Kitty Ernst Award and The Varney Participant Award, named for Helen Varney Burst. Only two recipients receive this national award each year and Nena was one of them.

While Nena is humble and doesn't like to talk about herself that much, Yu-jay loves to brag on his wife.

"Nena has a bachelor's from Davidson. She has a bachelor's of nursing from UNC-Chapel Hill, a master's of nursing from UNC, a PhD in nursing from UNC, and another master's-level equivalent nursing degree," he said, then added jokingly, "My kids are gonna be like, 'How come mom got all these degrees and you ain't got jack?!'"

Nena has gone on to become highly distinguished in her career, teaching at a major university nursing program, writing chapters in nursing textbooks, and serving as a family nurse practitioner, often serving in a free clinic for homeless women and children who reside at the Salvation Army's Center of Hope shelter in downtown Charlotte.

She currently is on faculty with the Frontier Nursing University, a Kentucky-based school that graduates more nurses and nurse midwives than any other school in the country. Much of their program is distance learning, allowing her to work from virtually anywhere in the country and only having to travel to Kentucky two or three times per year, giving her time to focus on her family.

Rosetta has been happily married for 20 years to Eric Woods, who has become one of Yu-jay's best friends. They live in Cornelius, NC, just outside of Charlotte, and have two children, aptly named Justice and Mercy. Justice is a senior at Community School of Davidson where he is one of the captains of the football team, a starter on the lacrosse team, an actor, solid student, and respected leader. Mercy is a sophomore at UNC-Greensboro, where she was admitted into the Honors College. She is also a graduate of the Community School of Davidson where Rosetta has worked for the past ten years as a teacher's assistant and receptionist.

When Yu-jay attended Charlotte Country Day, Jared went to another one of Charlotte's prestigious private schools, Providence Day, which is regarded as one of the best schools in the region, having received a Blue Ribbon School of Excellence Award, the highest award for an American school. However, Jared never fully enjoyed the private school experience, so he eventually transferred to North Mecklenburg High School, a county school twenty miles away from Providence Day. He took to the public school setting well and he lettered in multiple sports there, including basketball, track, wrestling, and football. He held state records for decades in the high jump and other track events.

After graduating, Jared went to St. Augustine College, a Historically Black College or University (HBCU) in Raleigh, NC, where he graduated with a degree in film and theater. He moved to L.A. after college for 7 years where he got small roles in some music videos, short films, and stage plays. He wrote a movie script about the Liberian civil war from a child's perspective that is registered with the Screen Writers' Guild.

Jared now lives in Boston and works as an Asset Protection Manager. He also owns a small film company called Sanai Films, named after his daughter, and he continues to pursue his passion for filmmaking. In the end, both of the boys found their paths.

Learn More

Sylvester Yarpah lives in Lynn, MA with his wife and three daughters, two of whom are in college in Massachusetts. One daughter is a senior and another is a freshman; his youngest is at home in middle school. Sylvester earned a Bachelor of Science in Management Studies in August 2010 from Cambridge College in Cambridge, MA. He has been working for Marriott Hotel in Boston since late 2003.

Uncle Moses still lives in Monrovia where he runs his own Tae Kwan Do school. He also uses his martial arts expertise to provide security for various business and government leaders and organizations.

Jamie Bowers, Yu-jay's first true friend in the U.S., graduated from one of the top public schools in the country, Myers Park High School, then earned a degree from Columbia International University. He spent 17 years in broadcasting and was part of an on-air team that won a prestigious Marconi Award from the National Association of Broadcasters for excellence in broadcasting. He later was recognized for contributing to an Emmy award-winning newscast. Currently, he serves as the Director of Communications for a U.S. Congressman. He is married to Lolly and they have three children.

"Yu-jay was focused on overcoming his circumstances and I was focused on becoming a successful broadcaster and we both did life together and supported those dreams," Jamie said. In the end both Yu-jay and Jamie ended up realizing their dreams.

Yu-jay's close friend, Carsten Weber, now lives in southern Germany in Aalen, Baden-Württemberg. He is a development engineer with a Ph.D. in physics. He is a brilliant man who remembers Yu-jay as a person "who was always very open to the world around him and someone who always wanted to try new things and embrace his surroundings."

Mary Ann Taylor continues her passion for helping Liberians. She remains a close friend of Rosetta, and is a busy grandmom. Her husband, Dr. Tom Taylor, retired after over two decades as an Economist at Duke Energy. He also taught at the Belk School of Business at UNC Charlotte.

Chris Martin retired from Charlotte Country Day School after over 20 years of teaching English and leading the department. He does some volunteer teaching at a local public school, is an avid writer, and enjoys being granddad.

Chris reflected on Yu-jay's experience. "He has lived the American Dream," he said, then added, "but he has also lived the Liberian American Dream."

Chris recalled Yu-jay keeping a daily schedule and writing down his personal goals in his pursuit of his personal dreams. He paused and made the point that it is less about setting goals and more about setting the right goals that

matters. He contrasted Yu-jay with a famous literary character.

"The young Jay Gatsby wrote down his goals and he
went after a rotten, spoiled American dream, whereas Yu-jay
did better."

Yu-jay definitely did better. He and Nena now live in
Charlotte with what has grown to be a family of six. Kyle is
their oldest, followed two years later by Olivia. Sophia was
born two years after that and then they had Gabriel, their
youngest.

His family has become a focal point of his life and he
takes his role as a husband and father seriously, receiving
high praise from Nena for his skill as a dad. He's also become

Learn More

a mentor to young men, including many
Liberians who have come to the United
States and need guidance in adjusting.
He and his fellow Liberian, Meanu Kayea,
began a mentoring group, meeting with
these teens and young adults, sometimes just to kick the
soccer ball around and other times to have small group conversations. It's one of the many ways Yu-jay has given back
to others.

One morning Yu-jay got a call requesting that he
return to his high school alma mater, Charlotte Country

Day, and deliver their convocation speech. At 8:00 a.m. on the morning of August 24, 2012, he stood before the student body, parents, and faculty and staff of the school and addressed them.[1] He told his story of life in Liberia and the war that changed all of their lives forever. He spoke of his new life in the United States and the challenges that had come with that. He talked about the generosity of others, like Mary Ann and Tom Taylor, and the value of relationships.

"People matter above anything else," he told them. "Living through the civil war taught me that possessions come and go. What matters most are the people in our lives—our family, classmates, friends, neighbors, and colleagues."

He spoke about how being different—a stranger in a strange land, a person who didn't fit the traditional mold in his new home—ended up being a blessing for him.

"I learned that different can be an asset. I found people who believed in a boy scarred by the horrors of war, but yet full of optimism." He added, "I learned the power and value of human relationships and our abilities to impact each other's lives."

Yu-jay was a boy who was born into hardship and poverty, then grew up in a world that had been thrown into violence and chaos. Despite the adversity, he became a young man who overcame all the odds, a person who was given a fresh start in a country with boundless opportunities. He took hold of this new hope and became a man who not only became a great personal success, but also invested richly in the lives of others.

He didn't set out to be a hero. He was just an asthmatic momma's boy who tried to survive a most horrific civil war, a brutal, bloody conflict that cost a quarter of a million people their lives. In the end, he not only survived, but he thrived. He is truly a hero, a role model, a champion. Rosetta's oldest son became America's son, an example to many, but he will always be the pride of Africa's beautiful land. He will always be Liberia's Son.

---

[1] Read the full text of his convocation speech in the appendix.

APPENDIX 1

CHARLOTTE COUNTRY DAY CONVOCATION SPEECH

Be the Best of Humanity

By Yu-jay Harris

Delivered at Charlotte Country Day School's Convocation on
August 24, 2012.

Mr. Reed, distinguished faculty and staff, board members, proud parents and the stellar class of 2013. It is more than an honor to be here today for this convocation.

It seems like just the other day I was sitting in your seats with my classmates listening to someone speak at my convocation. And to be honest, I don't even remember that day or what the speaker said. So I won't be offended if you all don't remember anything I say today 17 years from now. I'll just chalk it up to karma. But I do hope something I share will resonate with you at some point as you close this chapter in your lives next June, and embark on the great journey of life as adults.

Several months ago when Mr. Ball called and asked me to speak, two things happened after our chat. First, I felt greatly honored and excited that of all the graduates and influential people the school could have invited, I was extended this gracious invitation. But excitement was quickly replaced with me just freaking out. I empathized with Ms. J.K. Rowling, the author of the Harry Potter books, who during her 2006 graduation speech at Harvard, said that she had had weeks of fear and nausea at the very thought of speaking to the students. Fortunately for her, she ended up losing a lot of weight as a result and ultimately considered the ordeal a win-win. My sentiments exactly.

The challenge for me was trying to determine what to share with this very privileged class. Privileged to be at a school focused on developing critical thinkers with high character, and leaders taught to be committed to the communities in which you live. You are privileged to learn in a place where each member of the faculty and staff works tirelessly to live out and teach students the school's core values of educational excellence, character, community and service. And you are also privileged because you are a part of an environment replete with people from diverse backgrounds—different life experiences, nationalities, religions, socio- economic status, to name a few. So coming here to speak was no small undertaking. Fortunately, inspired by the story of the Little Engine that Could, I decided I could do this. And

Learn More

after much reflection, I settled on two things I want to share with you today. First, the story of how I came to be a student at this great institution. And secondly, three indelible lessons I learned here that continue to shape my life 17 years later.

Here's my story. About 18 months before I arrived on this campus in August 1992, I was living in Liberia, West Africa—where I was born and lived till I was 14. A quick history lesson on Liberia: It is a small English-speaking nation located on the West Coast of Africa. It was founded in 1847 by freed African America slaves who decided to return to Africa in pursuit of greater freedom and equality. Its government is modeled after the US and it has been a quasi-US colony since its formation.

Life was pretty good for me as a 13 year old boy living

in Monrovia, the nation's capital. My brother, Jared, and I had a relatively privileged life compared to many of our peers. My mother, Rosetta, here with me today, had worked very hard to give us opportunities she did not have as a young girl. I went to a Catholic college prep school, comparable to Country Day. We were surrounded by loving family and friends, and it seemed like every weekend was a family reunion. I played sports, namely table tennis and football (we call soccer here), and enjoyed video games. My brother and I had an Atari, which was like the Wii or Xbox of my youth—although I think most of the well-to-do kids had the Sega gaming system that launched in the early '80s.

But my journey to Country Day did not start when all was going well. It really began in June of 1990 when a civil war, that started six months earlier on the north central part of the country, spread like a wildfire and eventually reached our home in Monrovia some 250 miles away. We woke up one eerily calm morning to the reality that we were living in the middle of a warzone. Try to imagine living amidst what's happening in Syria, or what you saw in Libya last February, or even the American Civil War or any other war you're familiar with. And like residents faced with a wildfire, we were unprepared for survival in a civil war. We did not have stock piles of food and water, no flashlights with extra batteries, or much of anything. What little we had, we had to share with 13 other people who had fled their homes to take refuge with us. Life in a warzone meant we barely slept because of the incessant sounds of gunfire and sometimes large booms—likely hand or rocket propelled grenades or other bombs. We ate a morsel of food once every day, I think at 6:00 p.m., for several weeks before we were able to leave our home to take refuge in another city the war had already ravaged.

One of the scariest moments I recall was when 5 government soldiers—carrying M16 guns and looking terrified, as if they had seen multiple ghosts—kicked in our front door, began searching every room in the house and shouting, "Everyone get outside! Outside right now!" They lined us all up in front of the house and said they were going to kill us—for reasons never proffered. As we stood out there, frightened beyond measure, we were all thinking if these guys don't shoot us, who or whatever they were running from would certainly end our lives. Some of us were crying, while others turned to prayer asking God for a miracle, and yet others remained speechless, overtaken by the fear of impending death. And as the sound of gunfire drew closer, my mother, Rosetta, with great audacity, asked the soldiers to please let us back into the house so we could not get caught in any cross fire.

I recall, as a 13-year-old kid, standing out there with guns pointed at us and feeling like I saw my spirit and last breath flee my body leaving behind a shell of flesh and bones ready to be destroyed. I said a prayer and was ready to die. I would have the same feeling at two other times in 1990. Well, we were outside for about the longest 10 minutes of all of our lives, before the soldiers scurried away after ransacking our home leaving us feeling empty in so many ways. We would eventually see some of the jewelry, family pictures and other items they took from our house lying beside their bodies after they were killed by enemy soldiers.

The other two times I made peace with death at age 13 happened when I was thought to be a member of another group of rebel soldiers. Strangely, the rebels who started the civil war split up and started fighting each other and government forces. On both occasions, I was at the other end of semi-automatic machine guns wielded by kids younger and smaller in size than me. These young kids were called child soldiers and were often the most violent and evil of the soldiers because they appeared to lack any understanding of the consequences of their actions. They did not fully grasp what was happening when they shot or mutilated someone. They were brainwashed to believe each kill gave them some supernatural power as if playing a video game. Miraculously, each time I or my family members were in imminent danger, we were spared. Someone, always another soldier, would intervene on our behalf.

In a kind of "if you can't beat them, join them" move, we had some close family friends who joined one of the rebel groups to acquire some power and try to help their friends and loved ones. After a couple of months surviving in our house, with barely anything to eat, no water or electricity, living in a constant state of hyper fear, and having one-too-many close calls, we were rescued by one of these close friends who remembered us and got a handful of his men to come and find us. Our friend took us into refuge in the city where the main rebel leader had set up his government.

Throughout this experience, I was taking steps to become a student at Country Day. Those steps started with me living in the middle of a war zone, then living in the area run by rebel forces, and later being smuggled out of Liberia to the neighboring country, the Ivory Coast. We lived as refugees there for a couple of months and ultimately moved to Charlotte in April 1991 with the help of some amazing people—Mary Ann and Tom Taylor, both sitting here today. The Taylors were instrumental in orchestrating the opportunity for me to attend Country Day and getting my brother into Providence Day. Boo PD! I have nothing against PD. Just a little rivalry between by brother and me. Through them my family was blessed after seeing so much of the worst and most evil of humanity. We began to have hope again and experience the best of humanity. I now realize without the war, my family, most likely, would have never moved to this country and settled in Charlotte ultimately leading to my time here as a student. Our family is forever grateful for the difference the Taylors have made in our lives. Thank you Tom and Mary Ann for the challenges you overcame to touch the lives of people you did not even know.

When I arrived on this campus in August 1992, I was 18 months removed from the civil war but still haunted by the memories of the atrocities I saw and survived. My family had gone from a good life to a horrifying life in Liberia; to starting all over here in Charlotte. But for the three years I was a student here, I experienced more and more of the best of humanity as I made new friends and was embraced by this community. And as I reflected on my time here at Country Day and what I really learned, three salient lessons came to mind.

The first is that being different is good. It was very obvious I was different when I started classes. I was from a different continent, different country, had a different accent, a very different life experience, different socio-economic status, and more. I tried to mask whatever I could. I even got a book on how to speak Southern to help my accent. And I spent any money I had on buying the same fashion labels my friends wore. I wanted to fit in. But I quickly realized that my accent, my story, and life experiences were way more appreciated than my horrible attempt to sound Southern or anything else I tried to do to fit in.

My teachers valued my perspectives in the classroom. In an English course, I was able to share my experience living in a village when we read the classic novel Things Fall Apart by Chinua Achebe—a story set in a Nigerian village. In a US history course, I was able to share my perspective on the American civil war—having lived through one myself. On the soccer team, my coach appreciated my style of play and passion for the game—even though I was an asthmatic and could only go all out for about 5 minutes. My difference became an asset and remains so today. From applying to college, then graduate school, to interviewing for jobs, to making new friends, my difference has been a strong positive. I encourage each of you to get to know what makes you unique, embrace it and embrace the differences in others. You'll be surprised at the pleasant returns being different can deliver.

The second lifelong lesson I learned here is the importance of dreaming big. I did not know where my life was going after I left Country Day. Unlike many of you, college wasn't a certainty. I was not trying to follow in my parents footsteps to a certain college or a career path. I had survived a war and that was enough accomplishment for me. But while here, I got to know friends and parents who were accomplished or were pursuing paths to success in the corporate world, as civic leaders and community activists, religious leaders, doctors, lawyers, educators, and so much more. All of my friends were college bound and looking forward to careers in a variety of fields. Today, my five best friends from here are all graduates of some of the best colleges and universities in the US. One's a PhD physics professor in Berlin, two are electrical engineers, another is a pilot of a C130 Hercules military transport aircraft, and another buddy is a senior business advisory consultant in Dublin, Ireland. Observing their lives, I started to think big—for me. I say for me because thinking big is personal. While it can be influenced by what others are doing, it must be about you, your abilities, interests and passions. It is not about keeping up with anyone. It is about being your best self. I dreamed of going to college, getting a graduate degree, and working hard to achieve career success. I also dreamed of being a husband and father loved by my family and respected by others. And I have accomplished many of my early dreams and am still dreaming big today. Except that now, dreaming big has become less about what can acquire and more about how I can positively influence people's lives—giving back for all that's been given to me. As students at Country Day, I know you already have the intellectual capacity and ability to dream big. Your challenge, like mine, will be sustaining the effort it takes to accomplish your dreams as you encounter the vicissitudes of life beyond this school. Never give up—for in them you will find great reward.

The last, but most important lesson is that people matter above anything else. Living through the civil war taught me that possessions come and go. What matters most are the people in our lives—our family, classmates, friends, neighbors, and colleagues. And as a student here, this aphorism became my reality. Through their friendship and actions, my classmates, teachers, and the entire community made me believe I mattered. My English teacher and advisor, Mr. Chris Martin, took the time to get to know me and my story. He became a champion for me—believing in me. And he continues to do so today as my friend and mentor 17 years since my class with him. Ms. Ann Murphy, the college guidance counselor at the time, helped me realize that college was a very viable option. I think she even said that with my achievements here and my story, I probably could have gotten into any college or university I wanted to. By the time I graduated, I left Country Day knowing I had been a valuable member of this community. Because of my experience, I've made it one of my life's priorities to help others whenever possible. From directing a tutoring program that paired my Davidson classmates with less privileged elementary students in the community, to being an active big brother and mentor, to sponsoring five children through the humanitarian organization, World Vision, to recently co-founding a non-profit organization focused on mentoring adopted Liberian children who, like me, lived through the civil war, helping people improve their lives, has been a passion my wife and I share. It's a passion I encourage each of you to embrace.

As I close, let me state the obvious. Country Day was a launching pad for me. My personal faith in God grew here. I learned that different can be an asset. I found people who believed in a boy scarred by the horrors of war, but yet full of optimism. And I received a great education, in and out of the classroom, that set me on the path to realizing my big dreams of success and significance. Along the way, I learned the power and value of human relationships and our abilities to impact each other's lives.

I want say thank to some very special people. Mom, thank you for all the sacrifices you made to give your boys opportunities you never had. Mary Ann and Tom Taylor, thank you for adopting us and investing your time and resources in loving us like your own. Thanks to all my teachers and friends here who made my Country Day experience very memorable for all the right reasons. Thanks to my wife and partner, Nena, who daily embodies the very best of humanity to me. And thank you students for doing your best to listen to me today.

Lastly, to the students, be grateful for and treasure the special people in your lives—your parents, grandparents, teachers and other supporters in attendance today. Let them know you value them. And in whatever you do, where life takes you, try to positively influence the lives of others.

Thank you and God bless.

About the Author

Dave Verhaagen is the author or co-author of seven other books, a former broadcaster, and a licensed psychologist. He is married to Ellen and they have four young adult children, two of whom are siblings adopted from Liberia.

Other Books from Hero House

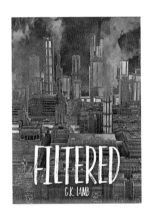

HeroHousePublishing.com